PERSONNEL

BUSINESS MANAGEMENT ENGLISH SERIES

Comfort, J. and N. Brieger
Marketing

Comfort, J. and N. Brieger
Finance

Brieger, N. and J. Comfort
Production and Operations

Brieger, N. and J. Comfort
Language Reference for Business English

Other ESP titles of interest include:

Brieger, N. and J. Comfort
*Business Contacts**

Brieger, N. and A. Cornish
*Secretarial Contacts**

Brieger, N. and J. Comfort
*Technical Contacts**

Brieger, N. and J. Comfort
*Social Contacts**

Brieger, N. and J. Comfort
Business Issues

Davies, S. *et al.*
*Bilingual Handbooks of Business
Correspondence and Communication*

McGovern, J. and J. McGovern
*Bank On Your English**

McKellen, J. and M. Spooner
*New Business Matters**

Palstra, R.
*Telephone English**

Palstra, R.
Telex English

Pote, M. *et al.*
*A Case for Business English**

* Includes audio cassette(s)

bme   *BUSINESS MANAGEMENT ENGLISH*

PERSONNEL

Nick Brieger
and
Jeremy Comfort

ENGLISH LANGUAGE TEACHING

Prentice Hall International

New York London Toronto Sydney Tokyo Singapore

First published 1992 by
Prentice Hall International (UK) Ltd
66 Wood Lane End, Hemel Hempstead
Hertfordshire HP2 4RG
A division of
Simon & Schuster International Group

© Prentice Hall International (UK) Ltd, 1992

Typeset by Keyboard Services, Luton
Printed and bound in Great Britain by Dotesios Ltd, Trowbridge

Library of Congress Cataloging-in-Publication Data

Brieger, Nick.
    Personnel / Nick Brieger and Jeremy Comfort
        p.   cm. – (Business management English series) (English
    language teaching)
    ISBN 0–13–093451–8
    1. Readers – Business.   2. English language – Business English.
    3. English language – Textbooks for foreign speakers.   4. Personnel
    management – Problems, exercises, etc.   5. Business – Problems,
    exercises, etc.   I. Title.   II. Series.   III. Series: English
    language teaching.
    PE1127.B86B69   1992
    428.6′4′02465 – dc20   91–18949
                                                                          CIP

British Library Cataloguing in Publication Data

Brieger, Nick
    Personnel. – (Business management English series)
    I. Title   II. Comfort, Jeremy   III. Series
    658.3

    ISBN 0–13–093451–8

1 2 3 4 5   96 95 94 93 92

Contents

KEY

GLOSSARY

Introduction

The Business Management English (BME) series comprises four professional content books:

Marketing
Finance
Production and Operations
Personnel

and also *Language Reference for Business English*, which acts as a language and communication reference for the other four titles.

Rationale

The rationale behind the BME series is to bring together training material in:

- key management disciplines,
- language knowledge, and
- communication skills.

The material is thus designed for:

- specialists who need to develop language and communication skills within their professional areas, and
- non-specialists who wish to extend their knowledge of management areas and develop their language and communication skills.

Personnel

Targets and objectives

This book is aimed at practitioners and students of personnel management: people who need to communicate in English within the increasingly international world of business management. More specifically the material is targeted at non-native speakers of English, with at least an intermediate level in the language, who need to:

- increase their effectiveness in reading and listening in this subject area,
- develop speaking and writing skills around this subject area,
- extend their active vocabulary of both specific personnel terms and more general business English, and
- transfer this knowledge of the language to their own work or study situation.

Organisation of materials

The book and its accompanying cassette are divided into Study Material, Key and Glossary.

STUDY MATERIAL

The Study Material comprises eight units, each of which is divided into two sections (A and B). Each section (A and B) is divided into two parts.

Part 1 is based on a reading task; Part 2 on a listening task. Each part contains the following activities:

1. *Warm-up*
   Questions designed as orientation for the following reading/listening task.

2. *Reading/Listening*
   An input text, together with a task.

3. *Comprehension/interpretation*
   Detailed questions about the input text.

4. *Language focus*
   Language practice exercises – a background explanation is given in *Language Reference for Business English*.

5. *Word study*
   Language exercises to develop professional, business and idiomatic vocabulary.

6. *Transfer*
   A speaking or writing communication task which encourages the user to transfer the information presented into his/her own field.

KEY

The Key comprises:

- Tapescripts of the listening extracts.
- Answers to the following activities from the Study Material:
  2. *Reading/Listening* task.
  3. *Comprehension/interpretation* questions.
  4. *Language focus* exercises.
  5. *Word study* exercises.
- Information for the communication activities, where needed.

GLOSSARY

A five hundred word dictionary of personnel management. The words have been selected on the basis of frequent usage in this subject area. They are not confined to words used in the book. Simple definitions are followed by an example of usage, where appropriate.

Using a unit – activities in each part

1. Warm-up

The questions here will help you to orientate yourself towards the tasks which follow. They encourage you to think about and discuss the subject area.

2. Reading/Listening

(i) *Reading*

Each text has been selected to focus on a key area of professional interest. There is always a task to perform either as you read or just after: this makes the process active. In order to develop your reading skills, you should:

- skim through the text to identify major themes, and
- scan through the relevant paragraphs to complete the task.

Then check your answers with the Key. If they are wrong, read the appropriate section again. The reading task is best done for homework/individual study; the answers can then be discussed in class.

(ii) *Listening*

Each text has been developed to focus on a key area of professional interest. Again there is always a task to perform as you listen to the cassette. In order to develop your listening skills, you should:

- listen all the way through first time, then
- listen again, stopping the cassette to write your answers.

Finally, check your answers with the Key.

3. Comprehension/interpretation

The questions have been developed to:

- check your detailed understanding, and
- encourage you to think more deeply about the subject.

You may need to read/listen again to answer the questions. If you are working in a class, discuss your answers. Finally, check the Key. As you will see, sometimes there is no 'correct' answer.

4. Language focus

This activity focuses on developing your language knowledge. You can do these exercises in class or on a self-study basis. Refer to *Language Reference for Business English* if you need further information. When you have completed an exercise, check the answers in the Key.

5. Word study

This activity concentrates on developing your word power. You can do this activity in class or on a self-study basis. The answers are in the Key. You may wish to check the Reading or Listening passage to see how the words are used.

6. Transfer

This activity develops your language and communication skills. It is best done in pairs or small groups. You will sometimes find additional information in the Key.

NOTE

The following distinction has been made to indicate what is missing in the exercises:

   _ _ _ _ _ _ _ _ _ _   one or more words
   _____   only one word

Acknowledgements

The authors would like to acknowledge the advice and support of colleagues at York Associates who gave them the time and space to complete and trial this book.

The publisher and authors would like to acknowledge with thanks the following copyright permissions:

Personnel Management – A New Approach, 4th edition, Derek Torrington and Laura Hall (1987), Prentice Hall.

Personnel Management, Gary Dessler (1988), Prentice Hall.

Management, 4th edition, James A. F. Stoner and R. Edward Freeman (1989), Prentice Hall.

Every effort has been made to trace and acknowledge ownership of copyright. The publishers will be glad to make suitable arrangements with any copyright holders whom it has not been possible to contact.

STUDY
MATERIAL

UNIT 1
The role of personnel management

Section A: What is personnel management?

Personnel management is both part of every manager's job as well as a separate staff function – one through which a personnel director assists all managers in important ways.

Part 1: Key aspects of personnel management

1 Warm-up

1.1 What are the purposes of personnel management?
1.2 What are the key elements of personnel management?

2 Reading

As you read, complete Chart 1.1 using the information in the text.

The work of personnel specialists varies between human resources management and personnel management. These are not different phrases with the same meaning, but different emphases in the work that all such specialists undertake. Personnel management is directed mainly at the organisation's employees; human resources management at management needs for human resources (not necessarily employees).

What, then, are the functions of the personnel specialist? According to one expert, 'The direct handling of people is, and always has been, an integral part of every line manager's responsibility, from president down to the lowest-level supervisor.' So all managers are, in a sense, personnnel managers, since they get involved in activities like recruiting, interviewing, selecting and training. Yet most firms also have a specialist department (personnel or human resources). So what are the duties of this manager? Before answering this question, let's start with a short definition of 'line' versus 'staff' authority.

Line managers are authorised to direct the work of subordinates – they're always someone's boss. In addition, line managers are in charge of accomplishing the basic goals of the organisation. Staff managers, on the other hand, are authorised to assist and advise line managers in accomplishing these basic goals. So personnel management is very much a part of every line manager's responsibility. These personnel management responsibilities include placing the right person on the right job, orienting, training and working to improve his or her job performance. In small organisations line managers may carry out these duties unassisted. But as the organisation grows, they need the assistance, specialised knowledge, and advice of a separate personnel staff.

Complete Chart 1.1 (an organigram) by writing in 'line' or 'staff', as appropriate.

Chart 1.1   Line and staff authority

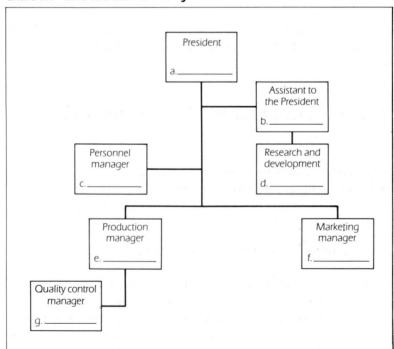

The personnel department provides this specialised assistance in the following areas:

- Job analysis (determining the nature of each employee's job)
- Planning manpower needs and recruiting job candidates
- Selecting job candidates
- Orienting and training new employees
- Wage and salary management (how to compensate employees)
- Providing incentives and benefits
- Appraising performance
- Face-to-face communicating (interviewing, counselling, disciplining)
- Developing managers

In addition, the personnel manager should know about:

- Equal opportunity and affirmative action
- Employee health and safety
- Handling grievances and labour relations

Above we have listed some of the activities of the personnel manager. However, we can also say that the personnel manager carries out three distinct functions, as follows:

1. *A line function.* First the personnel director performs a line function by directing the activities of the people in his or her department and in service areas, e.g. the plant cafeteria. In other words, he or she exerts line authority.

2. *A co-ordinative function.* Personnel directors also function as co-ordinators of personnel activities – as 'the right arm of the top executive to assure him that personnel objectives, policies and procedures are being consistently carried out.'

3. *Staff functions.* Staff functions to line management are the 'bread and butter' of the personnel director's job. These include assisting in the hiring, training, evaluating, rewarding, counselling, promoting and firing of employees at all levels.

3 *Comprehension/interpretation*

3.1 What difference between human resource management and personnel management is mentioned in the text?

3.2 What personnel activities are all managers involved in?

3.3 What three personnel functions are mentioned in the text?

3.4 To whom does the personnel manager provide each of these functions?

4 Language focus

4.1 Present passive verb forms (see Unit 22 in *Language Reference for Business English*)

Look at the following extracts taken from the Reading passage:

> 'Personnel management *is directed* mainly at the organisation's employees.'
> 'Line managers *are authorised* to direct the work of subordinates.'
> 'Personnel objectives, policies and procedures *are being* consistently *carried out*.'

Now put the following active sentences into the passive. Include **by** + the agent where appropriate and make any necessary changes to the word order. The first one has been done for you.

1. All personnel specialists have to undertake both human resources management and personnel management.
   Both human resources management and personnel management have to be undertaken by all personnel specialists.
2. At present we are assessing the organisation's manpower needs.
3. We can consider all managers as personnel managers.
4. Next week we are offering a seminar on delegation.
5. The MD is still considering the new appraisal scheme. We expect to introduce it later this year.
6. The personnel manager's responsibilities include orienting, training and working to improve job performance.
7. The line managers will be advising the personnel manager during the evaluation.
8. In small organisations, line managers may carry out personnel duties unassisted.

Now complete the sentences below by choosing an appropriate verb from the list and putting it into the correct present passive form:

raise   ask   consult   involve   make redundant

1. John expected _ _ _ _ _ _ _ _ _ _ about the new appraisal scheme.
2. By _ _ _ _ _ _ _ _ _ _, John hoped to make his own contribution.
3. While _ _ _ _ _ _ _ _ _ _, John stated his reservations about the scheme.
4. He said, 'Let the questions _ _ _ _ _ _ _ _ _ _ now rather than later.'
5. After _ _ _ _ _ _ _ _ _ _, John received many letters of support.

4.2 Like versus as (see Unit 65 in *Language Reference for Business English*)

Look at the following sentences taken from the Reading passage:

> 'They get involved in activities *like* recruiting, interviewing, selecting and training.'
> 'Personnel directors also function *as* co-ordinators of personnel activities.'

Now complete the following sentences by putting in **as** or **like**:

1. Peter has just been promoted. Now he works _____ assistant sales manager.
2. We offer training courses in areas _____ written communication, time management and counselling.
3. _____ usual at this time of year, the personnel manager is going to talk about the new pay awards.
4. The new merit scheme will be _____ follows:
5. It is just _____ them to ask for a big pay rise.
6. The situation is exactly _____ I said earlier: high wage rises and low productivity.
7. The prize is something _____ an award for special performance.
8. We try to use PR consultants _____ Brent and Chapel.

5 Word study

The following word table contains some key words from the field of personnel. Complete the table (the first one has been done for you).

Verb	Noun
recruit	recruitment
_____	orientation
perform	_____
_____	analysis
benefit	_____
_____	evaluation
appraise	_____
_____	development
compensate	_____
_____	promotion

6 Transfer

As we have seen, personnel management is important to all managers. Now discuss with your colleagues the personnel mistakes that you don't want to happen in your organisation, for example:

- To hire the wrong person for the job.
- Your people not doing their best.

Part 2: Introducing the personnel team

1 Warm-up

1.1 What job functions would you expect to find in the personnel department of a medium-size autonomous organisation?

1.2 What job functions would you expect to find in the personnel department of a large integrated organisation?

2 Listening

Codix is a leading name in confectionery production in the UK with a large domestic and overseas markets for its products. These products include chocolates and sweets, as well as some savoury snack foods such as crisps and peanuts. In this section you will hear the personnel director of Codix giving a short presentation of his team and their functions. As you listen, draw the organisation structure of the personnel department in Chart 1.2.

Chart 1.2   The Codix personnel team

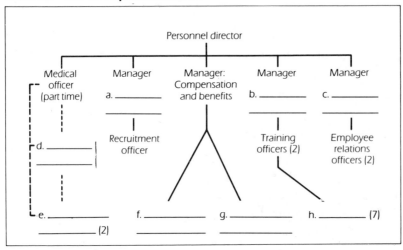

3 Comprehension/interpretation

3.1 What is the recruitment and selection manager responsible for?

3.2 The compensation and benefits manager handles two employee programmes. What are they?

3.3 What three areas are the training specialists in charge of?

3.4 What two broad activities does the safety officer perform?

4 Language focus

4.1 Describing the organisation (see Unit 69 in *Language Reference for Business English*)

Look at the following sentences taken from the Listening passage:

'The department *is headed* by me as personnel director.'
'And finally there is our employee relations manager who *is supported* by two employee relations officers.'
'She *is responsible for* maintaining contact within the community.'

Now use the information from the Listening passage to complete the following sentences. The first one has been done for you.

1. The personnel director *reports to* the president.
2. The personnel director _ _ _ _ _ _ _ _ _ _ for developing personnel policy for the company.
3. As you can see from the chart, the personnel department _ _ _ _ _ _ _ _ _ _ four sections.
4. The personnel director _ _ _ _ _ _ _ _ _ _ four section leaders, who are all managers.
5. Also _____ the personnel director are the medical officer, the safety officer and the nurses.
6. Each manager is _ _ _ _ _ _ _ _ _ _ of one of the following specialist areas: recruitment, compensation, training and employee relations.
7. The compensation and benefits manager _ _ _ _ _ _ _ _ _ _ a small team.
8. The benefits administrator _ _ _ _ _ _ _ _ _ _ to the compensation and benefits manager.
9. In addition to the _ _ _ _ _ _ _ _ _ _ company, Codix is at present planning to open a _ _ _ _ _ _ _ _ _ _ in the north-east of England.
10. The present personnel director will also _ _ _ _ _ _ _ _ _ _ of personnel policy in the new company.

4.2 Connecting and sequencing ideas (see Unit 67 in *Language Reference for Business English*)

Look at the following sentences taken from the Listening passage:

'*First of all*, just to run through the structure of the department.'
'*Then* there is the safety officer, who has two broad activities.'
'*Finally* there is our employee relations manager.'

Now use Chart 1.3 (Maslow's hierarchy of needs) to complete the written description by inserting appropriate sequence markers.

Chart 3.1   Maslow's hierarchy of needs

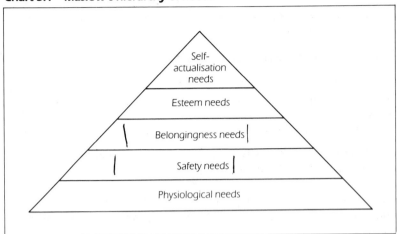

Maslow says that 1. _ _ _ _ _ _ _ _ _ _ an individual's physiological needs must be satisfied. These include the need for air, water, food and sex. 2. At_ _ _ _ _ _ _ _ _ _, an individual's safety needs must be satisfied. This means that the individual must feel safe and free from fear and threat. 3. _ _ _ _ _ _ _ _ _ _ that come the belongingess needs – the need for love, affection, feelings of belonging and, 4. _ _ _ _ _ _ _ _ _ _, human contact. 5. _ _ _ _ _ _ _ _ _ _ fulfilled their belongingness needs, individuals next need to satisfy their esteem needs. These include the following four needs: 6. _ _ _ _ _ _ _ _ _ _ self-respect, 7. _ _ _ _ _ _ _ _ _ _ self-esteem, 8. _ _ _ _ _ _ _ _ _ _ achievement and 9. _ _ _ _ _ _ _ _ _ _ respect from others. 10. _ _ _ _ _ _ _ _ _ _ step is to satisfy the self-actualisation needs – those needs which enable individuals to grow, to feel fulfilled and realise their potential. But 11. _ _ _ _ _ _ _ _ _ _ moving on to these higher level needs, the lower level needs must 12. _ _ _ _ _ _ _ _ _ _ be satisfied. An organisation must, therefore, 13. _ _ _ _ _ _ _ _ _ _ pay a wage sufficient to feed, shelter and protect employees and their families; in addition it must also provide a safe working environment 14. _ _ _ _ _ _ _ _ _ _ offering the employees incentives for developing self-esteem, belongingness and self-actualisation.

5 Word study

The following word table contains some more key words from the field of personnel.
Complete the table.

Verb	Noun concept	Noun person
_____	application	_____
instruct	_____	instructor
_____	_____	representative
_____	pension	_____
provide	_____	provider
_____	specialisation speciality (Br.E.) specialty (Am.E.)	_____
_____	_____	organiser
advise	_____	adviser/advisor

6 Transfer

As you heard in the Listening section, the position of training and development
manager at Codix is vacant. Draft an advertisement for a national newspaper. Your
advertisement should include:

- Information about Codix
- Information about the job
- Requirements from applicants (education, qualifications, career back-
  ground)
- Remuneration package
- How to apply

Section B: Personnel management philosophy

People's attitudes are always based in part on the basic assumptions they make,
and this is especially true with regard to personnel management. The basic
assumptions you make about people, such as whether they can be trusted, whether
they dislike work, and how they should be treated, comprise your philosophy of
personnel management. And every decision you make – the people you hire, the
training you provide, the benefits you offer – reflects (for better or worse) this basic
philosophy.

Part 1: Developing you personnel management philosophy

1 Warm-up

1.1 What aspects are likely to influence a person's (or personnel manager's) initial philosophy?

1.2 By what is this initial philosophy likely to be subsequently influenced?

2 Reading

In the text you will find two sets of assumptions:

1. Theory X, which states that workers cannot be trusted to work, and Theory Y, which states that people do not have an aversion to work.

2. System I and System IV, developed by Rensis Likert, looks at the organisational system. System I states that managers mistrust subordinates, while System IV states that managers have confidence in workers.

At present the assumptions are mixed up. Complete Charts 1.4 and 1.5 by writing in the appropriate theory or system to which they belong. The first one has been done for you.

So how do you go about developing a personnel management philosophy? To some extent, it is preordained. There is no doubt that a person brings to a job an initial philosophy based on his or her experiences, education, and background. But it doesn't have to be set in stone. It is a philosophy which should and will continually evolve as the person accumulates new knowledge and experiences. Let's therefore discuss some of the factors that will influence your own evolving philosophy.

INFLUENCE OF TOP MANAGEMENT'S PHILOSOPHY

One of the things molding your personnel philosophy will be that of your employer's top management. While top management's philosophy may or may not be stated, it is usually communicated by their actions and permeates every level and department of the organisation. For example, here is part of the personnel philosophy of Edwin Land, founder and former chief executive officer of the Polaroid Corporation:

> to give everyone working for the company a personal opportunity within the company for full exercise of his talents – to express his opinions, to share in the progress in the company as far as his capacity permits, and to earn enough money so that the need for earning more will not always be the first thing on his mind. The opportunity, in short, to make his work here a fully rewarding and important part of his life.

What sort of impact does a philosophy like this have? For one thing, all personnel policies and actions at Polaroid flow directly or indirectly from Land's basic aims. For example, there is a top-level personnel policy committee. It is a committee consisting of top corporate officers and is chaired by a senior vice-president, and members of the personnel department serve as staff, providing advice to the committee. The existence of this high-powered committee reflects the company's commitment to Land's personnel philosophy. And its existence helps ensure that all Polaroid personnel policies and practices – such as in the areas of training, promotions, and layoffs – also reflect this basic philosophy.

INFLUENCE OF YOUR OWN BASIC ASSUMPTIONS ABOUT PEOPLE

Your personnel management philosophy will also be influenced by the basic assumptions you make about people. For example, Douglas McGregor distinguishes between two sets of assumptions that he classified as Theory X and Theory Y. He says that the assumptions listed in Chart 1.4 hold.

Chart 1.4

1. The average human being does not inherently dislike work. (Y)
2. The average human being prefers to be directed and wishes to avoid responsibility. ( )
3. People are motivated best by satisfying their higher-order needs for achievement, esteem, and self-actualisation. ( )
4. The capacity to exercise a relatively high degree of imagination, ingenuity, and creativity in the solution of organisational problems is widely, not narrowly, distributed in the population. ( )
5. The average human being has an inherent dislike of work and will avoid it if he can. ( )
6. External control and the threat of punishment are not the only means for bringing about effort towards organisational objectives. ( )
7. The average human being learns, under proper conditions, not only to accept but also to seek responsibilities. ( )
8. Because of the human characteristic of dislike of work, most people must be coerced, controlled, directed and threatened with punishment to get them to put forth adequate effort. ( )

Rensis Likert says that assumptions like these manifest themselves in two basic types or systems of organisations, which he calls System I and System IV. He says that the assumptions listed in Chart 1.5 hold.

Chart 1.5

1. Management is seen as having no confidence or trust in subordinates. **(I)**
2. Workers are motivated by participation and involvement in decision-making. (   )
3. Subordinates are forced to work with fear, threats and punishment. (   )
4. Decision-making is widely dispersed and decentralised. (   )
5. There is widespread responsibility for control, with the lower echelon fully involved. (   )
6. There is extensive, friendly superior–subordinate interaction. (   )
7. The bulk of decisions and the goal-setting of the organisation are made at the top. (   )
8. Management is seen as having complete confidence and trust in subordinates. (   )
9. Control is highly concentrated in top management. (   )

In addition to factors like top management's philosophy and your assumptions, there is another factor – the need to motivate employees – that will affect your personnel philosophy.

MOTIVATION: A CENTRAL ISSUE

Motivating employees has always been a major concern of managers, and it's easy to see why. Managers get things done through others, and if you can't motivate your employees to get their jobs done, you are destined to fail as a manager.

This ability to motivate employees will be even more important in the future, since fundamental changes are taking place in the nature of work and the workforce. Productivity is down. Workers are becoming better educated and more concerned with their lifestyles. There is a shift from blue-collar to white-collar workers. And a multitude of new laws alter the techniques through which managers can ensure high production. It seems apparent that the days of the purely Theory X manager are numbered; managers will need new tools for tapping employees' higher-level needs – for motivating them.

So, as we've seen, developing a philosophy for personnel management is an evolutionary process influenced by experience, education, background and professional situation. The formulation put forward by Torrington and Hall* is that 'the philosophy of personnel management is a series of activities which first enables working people and their employing organisations to agree about the nature and objectives of the working relationship between them and, secondly, ensures that the agreement is fulfilled.'

*In *Personnel Management – A New Approach* (Prentice Hall, 4th edn, 1987, p. 11).

3 Comprehension/interpretation

3.1 What two factors will cause an individual's personnel management philosophy to evolve?

3.2 What evidence do we have from the text of Polaroid's commitment to Land's personnel policy?

3.3 McGregor's assumptions (Theory X and Theory Y) concern people; what do Likert's assumptions concern?

3.4 The author states that motivating employees will become more important in the future. He then mentions a movement in the workforce. What is it?

4 Language focus

4.1 Present simple versus present continuous (see Units 1 and 2 in *Language Reference for Business English*)

Look at the following sentences taken from the Reading passage:

'Fundamental changes *are taking place* in the nature of work and the workforce.'
'It *is* usually *communicated* by their actions and *permeates* every level and department of the organisation.'

Now complete the following sentences by putting the verb in brackets into the correct tense (simple or continuous) and correct form (active or passive), and making any necessary word order changes:

1. Theory X _ _ _ _ _ _ _ _ _ _ (state) that workers cannot be trusted to work.
2. At present the personnel policy committee _ _ _ _ _ _ _ _ _ _ (consist) of our top officers – which _ _ _ _ _ _ _ _ _ _ (show) our commitment to our employees.
3. If we _ _ _ _ _ _ _ _ _ _ (look) at the statistics, we can see that workers _ _ _ _ _ _ _ _ _ _ (become) better-educated and more concerned with their lifestyles.
4. At present we _ _ _ _ _ _ _ _ _ _ (work) on a policy to give everyone a personal opportunity for self-fulfilment.
5. Our employees definitely _ _ _ _ _ _ _ _ _ _ (feel) that they _ _ _ _ _ _ _ _ _ _ (belong) in this organisation.
6. The problem of redundancies hardly ever _ _ _ _ _ _ _ _ _ _ (discuss) here.
7. A: Have you got the appraisal forms?
   B: Not yet. They still _ _ _ _ _ _ _ _ _ _ (type up).
8. A: Any new developments?
   B: Yes, we just _ _ _ _ _ _ _ _ _ _ (run) a series of seminars on quality management.
9. I'm sorry but I _ _ _ _ _ _ _ _ _ _ (not agree) with the new personnel policy.
10. Just look at what _ _ _ _ _ _ _ _ _ _ (happen) in the service sector!

4.2 Be (see Unit 23 in *Language Reference for Business English*)

Look at the following sentences taken from the Reading passage:

> '*It is* a philosophy which should and will continually evolve as the person accumulates new knowledge and experiences.'
> '*There is* a shift from blue-collar to white-collar workers.'

Now complete the following sentences by putting in **it, they** or **there** with an appropriate tense of the verb **to be.**

1. In the meeting last week _ _ _ _ _ _ _ _ _ a lot of discussion about developing a personnel management philosophy.
2. In my opinion _ _ _ _ _ _ _ _ _ no doubt that a person brings to a job an initial philosophy based on his or her experiences, education, and background.
3. However, in a person's life _ _ _ _ _ _ _ _ _ always time to make changes.
4. In fact _ _ _ _ _ _ _ _ _ never too soon to evaluate one's performance.
5. Up to now _ _ _ _ _ _ _ _ _ (not) an official statement from management, but _ _ _ _ _ _ _ _ _ likely that one will be made in a few days.
6. _ _ _ _ _ _ _ _ _ my objective to give everyone in this company a personal opportunity to develop their talents.
7. In the future _ _ _ _ _ _ _ _ _ many opportunities; _ _ _ _ _ _ _ _ _ yours to seize.
8. For those of you joining the company _ _ _ _ _ _ _ _ _ a time and a place for everything.
9. _ _ _ _ _ _ _ _ _ a company I know where personal initiative is not welcomed; _ _ _ _ _ _ _ _ _ not this one.
10. _ _ _ _ _ _ _ _ _ all very well for you to ask for more money, but have you really earned it?
11. In the final analysis _ _ _ _ _ _ _ _ _ what you do that counts, not what you say.
12. Well, _ _ _ _ _ _ _ _ _ high time we went back to work.

5 Word study

On the left are ten words taken from the text. On the right are their opposites. Link each word to its correct opposite.

1. doubt		a.	reward
2. initial		b.	insufficient
3. permit		c.	minor
4. existence		d.	certainty
5. capacity		e.	superior
6. punishment		f.	prohibit
7. accept		g.	final
8. adequate		h.	inability
9. subordinate		i.	reject
10. major		j.	absence

6 Transfer

Theory X and Theory Y represent two extremes of belief, and naturally there are points between. What are your beliefs about people?

Part 2: Motivation – a central issue?

1 Warm-up

1.1 Think of your own job or studies. What tasks are you motivated to do well? Can you account for this?
1.2 What job characteristics have motivational properties?

2 Listening

Philip Bradshaw, the personnel director of Codix, a leading producer of confectionery in the UK, is a member of the Association of Personnel Managers (APM). This professional organisation holds both national and local meetings for personnel specialists. These meetings are of different types – some are round-table discussions, some presentations, and some formal dinners with guest speakers. Philip is the chairman of the northern branch. This evening there is a round-table discussion entitled 'Motivation – a central issue?', and Philip is going to introduce the subject and chair the discussion.

You are a member of the audience. Complete Chart 1.6 about motivation.

Chart 1.6

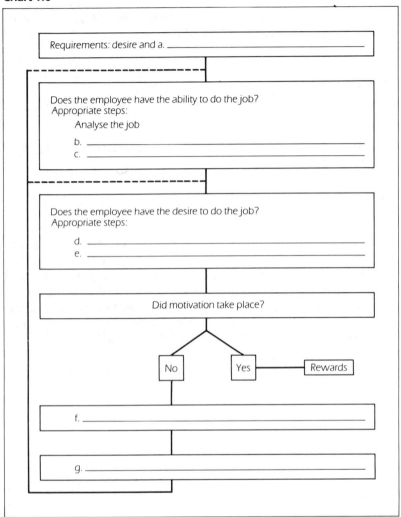

Requirements: desire and a. _____

Does the employee have the ability to do the job?
Appropriate steps:
  Analyse the job
  b. _____
  c. _____

Does the employee have the desire to do the job?
Appropriate steps:
  d. _____
  e. _____

Did motivation take place?

No   Yes —— Rewards

f. _____

g. _____

3 Comprehension/interpretation

3.1 Motivation derives from _____ to achieve the target and desire for the _____. What are the missing words?

3.2 When hiring people, what two characteristics should you, as personnel manager, look out for?

3.3 What two non-financial incentives did Philip mention?

3.4 If motivation does not take place, what three steps might a personnel manager take?

4 Language focus

4.1 Scale of likelihood (see Unit 80 in *Language Reference for Business English*)

Look at the following sentences taken from the Listening passage:

'You are *bound to* have all done your reading of . . . Maslow and Alderfer, Herzberg and Vroom.'

'Unless she also thinks there is *a reasonable chance*, unless she thinks it is *likely that* she can, in fact, make sales of £250,000.'

'You *may* need a change in selection standards.'

The table below consists of ten statements in the present tense + a degree of likelihood for each statement. For each statement, write the appropriate sentence so that each is a future forecast. The first one has been done for you.

	Certain	Probable	Possible	Improbable	Impossible
1. Our personnel policies have a major impact on individual performance				✓	
2. These policies affect the desire of employees to stay or leave	✓				
3. Our culture enhances or decreases an individual's performance			✓	–	
4. A creative, unconventional person fits into this culture					✓
5. Our type of culture motivates certain types of individual		✓			
6. Our pension plans attract some of our employees			✓		
7. Employees have lifetime loyalty to this company				✓	
8. The changes in working climate have an effect on the employees	✓				
9. Employees expect the management to improve benefits		✓			
10. We reward all individuals equally					✓

1. *Our personnel policies are unlikely to have a major impact on individual performance.*
   It is unlikely that our personnel policies will have a major impact on individual performance.

4.2 Expressions of clock time (see Unit 62 in *Language Reference for Business English*)

Look at the following sentences taken from the Listening passage:

> '*It's just gone eight* and so I'd like to welcome you all to our round-table discussion.'
> 'We will divide the evening into two sessions of *roughly one hour* each, with a break for *half an hour* at *around 9 o'clock*.'

Are the following expressions right or wrong? If wrong, what is the correct form?

1. I'll be back in a half hour.
2. It takes one and a half hour.
3. The meeting starts 3 o'clock.
4. The meeting starts at half past three o'clock.
5. The meeting starts at ten to four.
6. The train arrived at three past nine.
7. The train arrived at five past nine.
8. I'll finish it by seven o'clock p.m.
9. We'll leave at three thirty.
10. We'll leave at fifteen thirty.

5 Word study

The following word table is based on nouns and related adjectives. Complete the table by inserting the missing words.

Noun	Adjective
variety	_____
contribution	_____
administration	_____
_____	possible
example	_____
ability	_____
essence	_____
_____	important
_____	basic
_____	financial
_____	corrective
action	_____

6 *Transfer*

Describe a job in your organisation or an aspect of your study programme and write a short report suggesting how it could be redesigned to improve its motivational content. Your report should include:

- a description of the present situation,
- the problems arising from the present situation,
- your suggestion for change, and
- your evaluation of the improvement.

UNIT 2
Job analysis

Section A: The nature of and steps in job analysis

Job analysis is the process of collecting and analysing information about the tasks, responsibilities, and the context of jobs. The objective of job analysis is to report this information in the form of a written job specification, and sometimes, additionally, in the form of a person specification.

Part 1: The six steps in job analysis

1 Warm-up

1.1 What is the difference between an organisation chart or organigram and a job analysis?

1.2 For what personnel management activities can the job analysis be used?

2 Reading

Listed below are the six headings for the six steps in the text.

Collect job analysis information
Develop a job description and job specification
Determine the use of job analysis information
Select representative positions to be analysed
Collect background information
Review the information with the participants

As you read, select the heading that best describes the step and write it in the space provided. After you have read the text, complete Chart 2.1 using the information provided.

STEPS IN JOB ANALYSIS
The six steps in doing a job analysis are as follows:

Step 1. _____

Start by identifying the use to which the information will be put, since this will determine the type of data you collect and the technique you use to collect them.

There are many methods for collecting job analysis data; they range from qualitative interviews to highly quantified questionnaires. Some techniques – like interviewing the employee and asking the person what the job entails and what his responsibilities are – are uniquely suited for uses like writing job descriptions and selecting employees for the job. Other job analysis techniques such as position analysis questionnaires do not provide descriptive information for job descriptions, but do provide numerical ratings for each job; these can then be used to compare jobs with one another for compensation purposes. Your first step should therefore be to determine the use of the job analysis information. Then you can decide how to collect the information.

Step 2. _____

Next, review available information such as organisation charts, process charts, the job descriptions. Organisation charts show you how the job in question relates to other jobs and where it fits in the overall organisation. The organisation chart should identify the title of each position and, by means of its interconnecting lines, show who reports to whom and with whom the job incumbent is expected to communicate.

A process chart provides you with a more detailed understanding of the flow of work than you can obtain from the organisation chart alone. In its simplest form, a process chart shows the flow of inputs to and outputs from the job under study. In Chart 2.1, the inventory control clerk is expected to receive inventory from suppliers, take requests for inventory from the two plant managers, and provide requested inventory to these managers, as well as information to these managers on the status of in-stock inventories.

Chart 2.1   Process chart for analysing a job's work flow

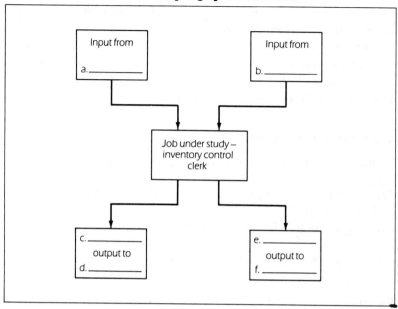

Finally, the existing job description, if there is one, can provide a good starting point from which to build your revised job description.

Step 3. _____

This step is necessary where many similar jobs are to be analysed and where it is too time-consuming to analyse, say, the jobs of all assembly line workers.

Step 4. _____

Your next step is to gather data on job activities, required employee behaviours, working conditions and human requirements (like the traits and abilities needed to perform the job). For this, you would use one or more of the job analysis techniques discussed in the listening section of this unit.

Step 5. _____

The job analysis provides information on the nature and functions of the job, and this information should be verified with the worker performing the job and the person's immediate supervisor. Verifying the information will help to determine if it is factually correct, complete, and easily understood by all concerned. And this 'review' step can help gain the person's acceptance of the job analysis data you collected by giving that person a chance to modify your description of the activities he or she performs.

Step 6. _____

In most cases, these concrete outcomes of the job analysis are typically developed next. The first is a written statement that describes the activities and responsibilities of the job, as well as important features of the job such as working conditions and safety hazards. The second summarises the personal qualities, traits, skills, and backgrounds required for getting the job done, and it may be either a separate document or on the same document as the job description.

3 Comprehension/interpretation

3.1 Which technique of job analysis is most appropriate for preparing a job description?

3.2 From which source would the job analyst expect to find information about communication networks?

3.3 With which two people should the job analyst review the information gathered?

3.4 What four areas does the job specification cover?

4 Language focus

4.1 Verb . . . *ing* (see Unit 12 in *Language Reference for Business English*)

Look at the following extracts taken from the Reading passage:

'The six steps in *doing* a job analysis are as follows.'
'Some techniques – like *interviewing* the employee . . .'
'*Verifying* the information will help to determine . . .'

Complete the text below by choosing the appropriate verb from the following list and putting it into the correct form.

write	recruit	analyse	define
hire	show	supervise	identify
administer	train	prepare	develop

Before 1. _____ an employee, recruiters should have a clear idea of the new employee's activities and responsibilities. Thus, the job analysis must be developed as an early step in the recruitment process. After 2. _____ a specific job, a statement should be drawn up in 3. _____, 4. _____ the content and location of the job. This is the job description. 5. _____ an accurate job description is very important and involves 6. _____ all the duties that must be carried out. For a sales manager, a brief description might read: 'Duties include 7. _____, 8. _____ and 9. _____ sales staff; in charge of 10. _____ sales department. As well as a job description, recruiters should consider 11. _____ a hiring description, 12. _____ the background, experience and skills required.

4.2   Reported questions (see Unit 37 in *Language Reference for Business English*)

Look at the following sentences taken from the Reading passage:

> 'Some techniques – like interviewing the employee and asking the person *what the job entails and what his responsibilities are* . . .'
> 'Organisation charts show you *how the job in question relates to other jobs and where it fits in the overall organisation.*'
> 'The organisation chart should . . . show *who reports to whom, and with whom the job incumbent is expected to communicate.*'

Change the following direct questions into reported questions by using the information given. The first one has been done for you.

1. How does this job relate to other jobs?
   The organisation chart shows *how this job relates to other jobs.*
2. How did the job fit into the overall organisation?
   The organisation chart showed _____ .
3. How has the work flowed?
   The process chart showed _____ .
4. Who has been receiving inventory from the suppliers?
   The process chart shows _____ .
5. What other information did we need?
   The existing job description showed _____ .
6. What are the activities and responsibilities of the job?
   The written job description will show _____ .
7. What qualities, skills and backgrounds did the applicant have to have?
   The person specification identified _____ .
8. When will the recruitment take place?
   Our sales manager decided last week _____ .
9. Have we completed the job analysis?
   The sales manager wanted to know _____ .
10. Why is it taking so long to analyse all the data?
    The sales manager asked _____ .

5 *Word study*

The following word table contains synonyms – words with the same or very similar meanings. Link the word on the left with its synonym on the right.

1. methods	a. decide
2. data	b. opportunity
3. collect	c. choose
4. position	d. modify
5. identify	e. techniques
6. revise	f. results
7. determine	g. gather
8. select	h. job
9. entail	i. characteristics
10. outcomes	j. information
11. requirements	k. needs
12. verify	l. show
13. chance	m. check
14. features	n. dangers
15. hazards	o. needs

6 *Transfer*

We saw in the above text that interview and questionnaire are two methods of collecting data. As a result of the restructuring of your organisation, you are going to carry out a job analysis on twenty-five plant supervisors in five factories. The question for your personnel management team is who should perform the job analysis. The possibilities are:

- the supervisor of the job holder
- the personnel officer
- the job holder
- outside technical expert

Part 2: Collecting job analysis information

1 *Warm-up*

1.1   Which job analysis method do you think is most useful for determining the duties and responsibilities of a job?

1.2   Which job analysis method do you think is quick and efficient for obtaining information from a large number of employees?

2 Listening

In this section you will hear an extract from a job analysis interview between Arthur Brent, a production supervisor at Codix, and the company's job analyst. As you listen write the analyst's notes in Chart 2.2.

Chart 2.2   Employee interview notes

General

Employee name: Arthur Brent

Present job title: _____

Department: _____

Major duties

1. To ensure that packaging work meets with the requirements.
2. _____
3. To instruct the packaging team about what to do.
4. _____
5. To review their work – to ensure it meets the specifications.
6. _____
7. To make sure that they've got enough packaging material at the beginning of each shift.

Place of work

Normally on _____

Occasionally called to _____ or to _____

Job conditions

	Acceptable	Unacceptable
Noise	☐	☐
Dirt	☐	☐
Heat	☐	☐

Demands of job

Which tasks cause particular stress?

1. _____
2. _____

3 Comprehension/interpretation

3.1 What subject does the job analyst want to postpone to another meeting?
3.2 Which other method of job analysis has Codix already used?
3.3 Which two people does Arthur contact in the event of a personal accident?
3.4 How does Arthur feel at the end of a shift?

4 Language focus

4.1 Questions (see Unit 38 in *Language Reference for Business English*)

Look at the following sentences taken from the Listening passage:

> *'So, what exactly is your job title?'*
> *'What exactly do you mean?'*
> *'And do you feel tired at the end of a shift?'*

Now complete the dialogue with an appropriate question. The first one has been done for you.

A: *Where do you work?*
B: In the packaging department.
A: _ _ _ _ _ _ _ _ _ _?
B: I started at Codix seven years ago.
A: _ _ _ _ _ _ _ _ _?
B: I've been a supervisor for three years now.
A: _ _ _ _ _ _ _ _ _?
B: Well, I ensure that our packaging work meets with the requirements.
A: _ _ _ _ _ _ _ _ _?
B: I report to the plant manager.
A: _ _ _ _ _ _ _ _ _?
B: There are five of us in our team.
A: _ _ _ _ _ _ _ _ _?
B: We use the packaging machine over there.
A: _ _ _ _ _ _ _ _ _?
B: Yes, it breaks down from time to time.
A: _ _ _ _ _ _ _ _ _?
B: Reppack repair it when it breaks down.
A: _ _ _ _ _ _ _ _ _?
B: No, nobody has had an accident recently?
A: _ _ _ _ _ _ _ _ _?
B: I think the last accident happened about two years ago.
A: Right, well thanks for your help.

4.2 **For** versus **during** (see Unit 63 in *Language Reference for Business English*)

Look at the following sentences taken from the Listening passage:

'I've been a supervisor *for* three years now.'
'I'm going to make some notes *during* the interview.'

Now complete the following sentences with **for** or **during**:

1. There's only been one breakdown _____ the last three years.
2. We couldn't get the machine repaired _____ a whole week.
3. I've never seen a problem like it _____ all the time that I've been here.
4. I asked the maintenance men how long the machine would be out of action _____.
5. They said that they thought they could mend it _____ the night shift.
6. So they worked on it _____ the whole night, but they couldn't mend it.
7. So they had to put in a replacement _____ the short term.
8. Then they contacted us _____ the morning to tell us that it would be out of action _____ at least a week.

5 Word study

The following word table has three columns – verbs in the first column, particles in the second column, and nouns in the third column. Draw lines to link each verb with one appropriate particle and one appropriate noun. The first one has been done for you.

Verb	Particle	Noun
fill	with	the plant manager
carry	after	Codix
meet	in	the problem
sort	at	the questionnaire
look	to	an interview
report	at	the notes
look	out	the requirements
start	out	the equipment

6 Transfer

As we have already said, questionnaires are a good method for obtaining job analysis information. The main thing to decide is how structured the questionnaire should be. At one extreme, some questionnaires are very structured checklists; at the other extreme, the questionnaire can be open-ended and simply ask the employee: 'describe the major duties of your job'. In practice, the best questionnaire often falls between these two extremes. Draft a questionnaire for the job analysis of supervisors at Codix. Your questionnaire should include questions about:

- major job duties
- less important job duties
- formal education/training needed for the job
- previous similar or related work experience necessary to do the job
- initiative required for the job
- errors likely to occur on this job
- lines of communication in the job
- disagreeable conditions of the job
- other comments

Remember that your questionnaire should balance open questions with closed questions. You can use some of the areas covered in the interview, if you want.

Section B: Job description and person specification

We said in section A that the objective of job analysis is to report the information collected in the form of a written job specification, and sometimes, additionally, in the form of a person specification. A job description is a written statement of what the job holder actually does, how he or she does it, and under what conditions the job is performed. This information is in turn used to write a person specification, which defines the human characteristics and experience required to do the job.

Part 1: The job description

1 Warm-up

1.1 What sections would you expect to find in a job description?
1.2 What style of writing should be used in job descriptions?

2 Reading

Read the following passage on writing job descriptions. As you read, complete Chart 2.3.

WRITING JOB DESCRIPTIONS

While there is no standard format you must use in writing a job description, most descriptions contain at least sections on:

1. Job identification
2. Context
3. Job summary
4. Job content
5. Performance standards
6. Working conditions

Job identification

The job identification section contains several types of information. The job title specifies the title of the job, such as production supervisor or training and development manager. The job code permits easy referencing of all jobs. Each job in the organisation should be referenced with a code, and these codes represent important characteristics of the job, such as the wage class to which it belongs. The date refers to the date the job description was actually written, and 'written by' indicates the person who wrote it. There is also space to indicate who the description was approved by.

Context

This section indicates where the job is to be carried out, e.g. in terms of location, plant, division, department, section. It also shows the job holder's relationships with others inside and outside the organisation. For the training and development manager at Codix it might look like this:

Reports to: personnel director
Supervises: training officers (2) and training instructors (7)
Works with: all department managers
Outside the company: training suppliers

Job summary

This section should describe the general nature of the job, listing only its major functions or activities. Thus the training and development manager:

- assesses the company's training needs
- plans, organises and evaluates training programmes to satisfy these needs
- provides managers with the leadership skills they need to do their jobs

Job content

This section should present a detailed list of the actual responsibilities and duties of the job. Each of the job's major duties should be listed separately, with one or two sentences then provided for describing each.

Chart 2.3

In the following job description for a training manager the content section has the following main headings:

1. Running courses
2. Running a training centre
3. Providing advice to line managers
4. Identification of the organisation's training needs and development of training plans
5. Liaison with external training providers
6. Evaluation of effectiveness of training

Now organise the following additional information under the appropriate heading by writing a number in the range 1–6 in the brackets:

a. To ensure that adequate trainers are available for the organisation's courses. (1)
b. To maintain and update a register of trainers and training organisations suitable for the organisation's training courses.(   )
c. To ensure adequate resourcing of the organisation's training centre – hardware, software and courseware. (   )
d. To review the efficacy of all training programmes through post-course questionnaires, interviews and feedback. (   )
e. To select the most effective suppliers based on the organisation's training needs. (   )
f. To devise training plans in line with identified needs. (   )
g. To ensure that the organisation's training courses run smoothly in terms of administration and training. (   )
h. To publish a programme showing the training programmes offered by the training centre. (   )
i. To administer the organisation's training budget. (   )
j. To work actively with the management team to identify the organisation's needs and priorities in terms of training. (   )
k. To evaluate suppliers in terms of their training effectiveness. (   )
l. To provide support within the organisation to troubleshoot problems and suggest training solutions. (   )

Performance standards

Some job descriptions also contain a standards of performance section. This basically states how well the employee is expected to achieve each of the main duties and responsibilities in the job description.

Because of the problems associated with setting standards, most managers soon learn that just telling subordinates to 'do their best' does not provide enough guidance. Here are some performance standards from the job description for a senior sales assistant:

Performance standards

There are two critically important areas:

1. *Sales volume*: minimum sales to the value of £400,000 over each six month accounting period.

2. *Relations with customers*:

   - Customers' queries answered immediately.
   - Customers always given a demonstration when they request this.
   - Delivery times arranged to meet both customer and delivery dept needs.
   - Complaints investigated immediately.
   - Customers assured that problems resolved as soon as possible.
   - Problems that cannot be dealt with referred immediately to manager.

Working conditions

The job description will also list any special working conditions involved on the job. These might include things like noise level, hazardous conditions, or heat. In addition this section will contain information on:

- working hours
- pay
- holiday entitlement
- other entitlements

PROBLEMS WITH JOB DESCRIPTIONS

The production of job descriptions is not without problems. These problems do not make job descriptions invalid, but it is important to be aware of them.

Sources of error

If the job analysis was collected from an insufficient number of sources, it may be incomplete or biased. The job analyst may also be unintentionally biased in his interpretation of the information that has been collected. The environment of job analysis may lead to errors in the analysis. Such factors as time pressures may cause the analysis. Such factors as time pressures may cause the collection and interpretation of information to be rushed; or it may be due to lack of interest/commitment on the part

of managers, supervisors and job incumbents; and distracting physical or environ-
mental conditions would be relevant here.

Appropriateness of job descriptions

Ungerson (1983) identifies a further set of problems relating to the appropriateness of
job descriptions:

1. Job descriptions are often seen as not appropriate for top management as these
   people should be free to map out their own territory and use their initiative.

2. Job descriptions are inflexible and they can be a hindrance to the development of
   organisations which are growing rapidly or changing technologically.

3. Job descriptions become out of date very quickly since there is always a drift in
   job content.

Ungerson meets these criticisms by arguing that flexibility can be built into the
structure and working of job descriptions, and that there should be plans for the
regular upgrading of job descriptions on an ongoing basis.

JOB DESCRIPTION GUIDELINES

Here are some hints for writing your job descriptions:

Be clear.   The job description should portray the work of the position so well that the
duties are clear without reference to other job descriptions.

Indicate scope.   In defining the position, be sure to indicate the scope and nature of the
work by using phrases such as 'for the department' or 'as requested by the manager'.
Include all important relationships.

Be specific.   Select the most specific words to show: (1) the kind of work, (2) the degree
of complexity, (3) the degree of skill required, (4) the extent to which problems are
standardised, (5) the extent of the worker's responsibility for every phase of the work,
and (6) the degree and type of accountability. Use action words such as analyse,
gather, assemble, plan, devise, infer, deliver, transmit, maintain, supervise, and
recommend. Positions at the lower levels of organisation generally have the most
detailed duties or tasks, while higher-level positions deal with broader aspects.

Be brief.   Brief accurate statements usually best accomplish the purpose.

Recheck.   Finally, check whether the descriptions fulfil the basic requirements, ask
yourself, 'Will a new employee understand the job if he or she reads the job description?'

3 Comprehension/interpretation

3.1 What five items of information should be included in the job identification section?

3.2 Why may it be difficult to describe performance standards?

3.3 For which category of personnel may job descriptions not be appropriate?

3.4 Which job positions need the most detailed specification of duties?

4 Language focus

4.1 Cause and effect (see Unit 77 in *Language Reference for Business English*)

Look at the following sentences taken from the Reading passage:

> 'Such factors as time pressures may *cause* the collection and interpretation of information to be rushed . . .'
> '*Because of* the problems associated with setting standards, most managers soon learn that just telling subordinates to 'do their best' does not provide enough guidance.'
> 'Job descriptions are often seen as not appropriate for top management *as* these people should be free to map out their own territory and use their initiative.'

Now rewrite the following sentences using the connector or construction given in brackets and make any other stylistic or grammar changes that you think are necessary. The first one has been done for you.

1. The task of selecting managers is difficult because the manager's job is complex. (phrase of cause)
   The task of selecting managers is difficult because of the complexity of the manager's job.
2. Selection of managers depends on accurate assessment because of the wide variety of skills used by managers. (clause of cause)
3. Organisations may hire experienced managers for different reasons. (verb of cause)
4. The organisation may recruit from outside because the talent does not exist within the organisation. (sentence connector)
5. Because it is frequently difficult to evaluate a manager's past performance, interviewers use other assessment tools. (phrase of cause)
6. Potential managers haven't yet had any work experience. Therefore they are difficult to recruit. (clause of cause)
7. Good managerial performance does not automatically result from good university or college performance. (verb of cause)
8. Since non-academic interests can provide some insights into managerial potential, many organisations look for evidence of extra-curricular managerial interest. (sentence connector)
9. Several managers normally interview a candidate because this increases the likelihood of making a good choice. (phrase of cause)
10. Different viewpoints reduce the risk of losing an effective manager because of one interviewer's bias. (clause of cause)

4.2　**All, each, every** (see Units 59 and 61 in *Language Reference for Business English*)

Look at the following sentences taken from the Reading passage:

'Include *all* important relationships.'
'*Each* job in the organisation should be referenced with a code . . .'
'The extent of the worker's responsibility for *every* phase of the work . . .'

How many correct expressions can you make by linking the phrases on the left with the nouns on the right? Draw lines to make the correct expressions.

	day
all	equipment
all the	machines
all of the	information
each	hour
each of the	employee
every	jobs
	work

Now complete these sentences with **all, each, every** or a compound:

1. _____ at the meeting agreed with the decision.
2. We have a management meeting _____ Friday.
3. _____ the managers thought that his appointment was a good decision.
4. You have _____ to win and nothing to lose.
5. In the interview you'll need about half an hour with _____ of the candidates.

5　*Word study*

The following verbs are used in the text to explain what the job description (or one of its parts) does, e.g the job title specifies the title of the job, such as production super-visor or training and development manager. What are the nouns from these verbs?

Verbs	*Nouns*
specify	_____
indicate	_____
describe	_____
present	_____
state	_____
list	_____
identify	_____
portray	_____
define	_____
summarise	_____
contain	_____
include	_____

6 Transfer

As a result of the restructuring of your organisation, a job analysis was carried out on twenty-five plant supervisors in five factories. An outside technical expert was brought in to conduct the analyses and draw up the job descriptions. The resulting descriptions were shown to the plant manager, who said that some of the supervisors had exaggerated their duties. In interviews, however, some of the supervisors claimed they were asked to carry out jobs that they should not be doing.

The question for your personnel management team is: should you ignore these controversies?

Part 2: Defining the human characteristics

1 Warm-up

1.1 When looking for trained personnel, what job or person specifications would you include?

1.2 What particular problems would you face when writing job or person specifications for untrained personnel?

2 Listening

In this section you will hear an extract from a discussion between a data processing manager at Codix and the employment manager. In line with company policy they are drawing up person specifications for various positions within the organisation. This meeting is to discuss the position of team leader within the data processing department, reporting to the project leader. As you listen, write in the missing requirements in Chart 2.4.

Chart 2.4   Person specification for the job of team leader

Physical make-up

Essential: ————————————————————————————————

Attainment

Preferred: 'O' level Maths   Essential: CSE Maths minimum

Preferred: *Either*
             Attendance at a programming course, in or out of school
             or
             Demonstrate some self-taught knowledge of programming

Essential: ————————————————————————————————

General intelligence

Essential: ————————————————————————————————

————————————————————————————————

Special aptitudes

Essential: Ability to relate to people
             Ability to form relationships quickly

Interests

Essential: ————————————————————————————————

Disposition

Essential: ————————————————————————————————

————————————————————————————————

Circumstances

Essential: Circumstances that ————————————————————————————

————————————————————————————————

3   Comprehension/interpretation

3.1   Where's the bottleneck in the data processing department?

3.2   What is the position below junior project leader?

3.3   What is the name of the person specification system used in Codix?

3.4   With whom has the data processing manager already discussed the human specifications for the post of team leader?

4 Language focus

4.1 Obligations and requirements (see Unit 78 in *Language Reference for Business English*)

Look at the following sentences taken from the Listening passage:

'Yes, they *must* dress in a "business-like" manner.'
'The person *has to* have good keyboard skills.'
'So the person *needn't* work every Saturday?'
'Yes, we *mustn't* have one of those slow analytical types in this job.'

Use the person specification table below to form fifteen sentences about the ideal applicant. The first one has been done for you.

	Necessary	Prohibited	Not necessary
Physical make-up			
1. Look tidy	✓		
Attainment			
2. Have a management qualification	✓		
3. An MBA			✓
4. Show good interpersonal skills	✓		
5. Be aggressive		✓	
General intelligence			
6. Be of above average intelligence	✓		
7. Be intellectual			✓
Special aptitudes			
8. Can communicate with all levels	✓		
9. See him/herself as a typical middle manager		✓	
Interests			
10. Be interested in developing people skills	✓		
11. An interest in technical aspects			✓
Disposition			
12. Show a logical approach to problem-solving	✓		
13. Seem prone to stress		✓	
Circumstances			
14. Have a secure family life	✓		
15. Live within this region			✓

1. *The applicant must look tidy.*

4.2   Have, have got and **get** (see Unit 29 in *Language Reference for Business English*)

Look at the following sentences taken from the Listening passage:

> 'What *'s* happened up till now is that we *'ve* promoted the analyst/programmers to junior project leaders.'
> 'Yes, I *'ve got* some notes on that here.'
> 'But last year we *got* eight new analyst programmers . . .'

Now complete the following dialogue with an appropriate verb in the correct form:

A: _ _ _ _ _ _ _ _ _ _ we run the interviews for the production post yet?
B: We still (not) _ _ _ _ _ _ _ _ _ the job specification.
A: I thought I _ _ _ _ _ _ _ _ _ _ seen it.
B: No, we _ _ _ _ _ _ _ _ _ _ the person specification, but the job description _ _ _ _ _ _ _ _ _ _ not come back from George.
A: But he _ _ _ _ _ _ _ _ _ _ it about a week ago, didn't he?
B: Well, in fact he _ _ _ _ _ _ _ _ _ _ it at the beginning of the week but he _ _ _ _ _ _ _ _ _ _ been pretty busy.
A: Really?
B: Yes, you know the new bottling machine that he _ _ _ _ _ _ _ _ _ last month.
A: I _ _ _ _ _ _ _ _ _ _ heard about it.
B: Well, apparently they _ _ _ _ _ _ _ _ _ _ a lot of problems with it. It (not) _ _ _ _ _ _ _ _ _ _ the right speed for our belts.
A: So, are they going to _ _ _ _ _ _ _ _ _ _ a replacement?
B: I _ _ _ _ _ _ _ _ _ _ to talk to him about that now.

5   Word study

We can form the opposite of an adjective by adding either a prefix (at the beginning), e.g. tidy – untidy, or by adding a suffix (at the end), e.g. useful – useless. What are the opposites of the following adjectives?

Adjective	*Opposite adjective*
systematic	_____
essential	_____
helpful	_____
interested	_____
patient	_____
applicable	_____
agreeable	_____
intelligent	_____
able	_____
careful	_____
appropriate	_____
logical	_____

6 *Transfer*

You have now looked at job analysis (using different methods of collecting data), and we have considered job description (key contents) and person specification (main areas). Write a job description and person specification for one of the following:

- Your instructor's job
- The job of one of your classroom colleagues

Depending on the time available, you should analyse the job either by interview (less time-consuming) or questionnaire and then design the job description and person specification according to the guidelines given in this unit. When you have completed your document, give it to your instructor or colleague for evaluation.

UNIT 3
Planning and recruiting

Section A: Forecasting personnel requirements

How do you plan for the openings that inevitably develop in your organisation? You could choose to wait for the opening to develop and then try to fill it as best you can. Most managers use this approach and it's probably effective enough for small organisations. But for larger firms (and for managers who want to avoid last minute scurrying and mistakes), some forecasting and planning are worthwhile.

Part 1: Manpower planning activities

1 Warm-up

1.1   What is the overall purpose of manpower planning?
1.2   What are the specific objectives of manpower planning?

2 Reading

As you read, complete Chart 3.1 using the information in the text.

MANPOWER PLANNING ACTIVITIES

What activities need to be carried out to make sure that the manpower resources are right? How do we find out at an early stage the number and types of employee that will be needed and make plans to ensure they will be available? Manpower planning activities centre around:

- forecast of future demand for manpower
- consideration of changes in manpower utilisation and the effect of this on manpower demand
- analysis of current manpower
- forecast of internal manpower supply
- forecast of external manpower supply
- reconciliation and feedback
- decisions and plans

Chart 3.1 shows these activities and their primary relationships. The manpower demand can be forecast using information from corporate plans or business plans, if these exist. Such plans express the organisation's activity in such terms as production figures, sales figures, levels of service and so on.

Manpower utilisation is an important factor which can affect the demand for manpower. The way that manpower is used affects, among other things, the number and type of employees required. The way that manpower is used can be changed in a number of ways, such as:

- the actual tasks performed, as these may be altered or added to
- the time spent on each task
- the level at which the tasks are carried out; that is, in whose job description the task is located

There are various reasons why manpower utilisation may be changed. Changes in manpower utilisation are often seen as synonymous with improvements in manpower utilisation in order to increase productivity.

Changes in manpower utilisation often involve negotiation, or at least consultation with trade unions. It would be naive to assume that management could decide on the most efficient way to utilise manpower and implement this directly. Changes in utilisation are also difficult to implement as they require lengthy planning, and also create a certain amount of upheaval before, during and after implementation. It is, therefore, more realistic to see manpower utilisation as an area that management should be primarily aware of and should improve where possible.

Having forecast the demand for manpower, taking into account any changes in the way manpower is to be utilised, the next step is to analyse the current supply of manpower. Current manpower can be analysed on overall terms, such as numbers of people in each occupation, or by age. The analysis of current manpower is essential as it provides a base from which to forecast the future internal manpower supply. It is also important for the formulation of career, succession, and redundancy plans.

Internal manpower supply forecasts attempt to predict future internal manpower based on trends of what has happened to internal manpower in the past. Manpower planners are concerned with trends of employees who leave the organisation, sometimes called wastage or turnover; but also with trends of internal employee movements. Trends from the past are projected into the future to simulate what will happen to the current manpower in, say, one or two years' time. This is the area of manpower planning where forecasting of internal manpower supply is usually looked at chiefly in statistical terms. There is, however, some interest in the behavioural aspects of this, for example consideration of the reasons for wastage.

A forecast of external manpower supply is needed if internal manpower supply is unlikely to meet manpower demand in any occupational areas. External manpower supply is, of course, particularly critical if a new plant or office is to be opened. External factors may also have an effect on current manpower wastage rates and the expectations of employees may be affected if a company offering similar employment at higher wages locates itself close by.

The supply and demand forecasts need to be balanced and reconciled, and this process necessitates feedback into previous stages of the process. Feedback, in fact, needs to be occurring throughout the whole process, and not just at this stage.

Manpower planning activities have been described here, for the sake of clarity, as a series of stages. In reality these activities are not carried out in a predetermined order, but to some extent at the same time so that information generated from each activity can be used continuously to inform the others. This feedback is vital if manpower planning is to have any practical value. For example, corporate objectives may need to be reconsidered if the analysis and forecast of manpower supply cannot meet the demand for manpower that has been derived from these objectives. Alternatively, the type of manpower employed or the utilisation of manpower may be reconsidered to see if the objectives may be met in another way.

Manpower decisions based on the manpower forecasts and their eventual balancing result in the production of manpower plans, which are action plans covering such areas as recruitment, training, productivity and personnel policies.

Chart 3.1 Manpower planning activities

Company objectives

Manpower utilisation

Analysis of manpower resources

a.

b.

c.

Current supply

d.

e.

Budget

Manpower plans

3 Comprehension/interpretation

3.1 Why are changes in manpower utilisation often introduced?
3.2 From what is the forecast of future internal manpower supply calculated?
3.3 What two areas are internal manpower supply planners particularly concerned with?
3.4 What two steps may a company have to take if it cannot satisfy its manpower demands?

4 Language focus

4.1 Relative clauses (see Unit 39 in *Language Reference for Business English*)

Look at the following sentences taken from the Reading passage:

'Manpower planners are concerned with trends of employees *who leave the organisation*, sometimes called wastage or turnover . . .'
'Manpower utilisation is an important factor *which can affect the demand for manpower*.'

Now combine the following sentences using a relative clause. You may need to make some small changes to the words and the word order to make your final sentence sound more natural. The first one has been done for you.

1. Human resources management is a management function. It deals with the recruitment, placement, training and development of a company's personnel.
   Human resources management is the management function which/that deals with the recruitment, placement, training and development of a company's personnel.
2. We need to select people. They must have the best potential for the job.
3. We saw some candidates last week. They all seem to have great potential.
4. We have decided to appoint John Casperton. At present he is working as a factory supervisor.
5. He is going to take over next month. Paul retires then.
6. We have made many placements. All of them have been a success.
7. Training room 101 is much too small. You intend to run the quality seminar there.
8. The training plan took four weeks to prepare. It has now been published.
9. We are going to send Peter back to college. He hopes to get a management qualification there.
10. Our managing director has proposed a personnel planning committee. You know his views on personnel well.

4.2   Adjectives versus adverbs (see Unit 48 in *Language Reference for Business English*)

Look at the following sentences taken from the Reading passage:

'*External* factors may also have an effect on *current* manpower wastage rates . . .'
'External manpower supply is, of course, *particularly* critical if a new plant or office is to be opened.'
'Each activity can be used *continuously* to inform the others.'

Complete the sentences with the correct form of the word given in brackets.

1. The manpower demand can be _____ forecast using information from corporate plans or business plans. (accuracy)
2. Manpower utilisation is a factor which can _____ affect the demand for manpower. (significance)
3. The way that manpower is used has a _____ effect on the number and type of employees required. (major)
4. There are _____ reasons why manpower utilisation may be changed. (variety)
5. We can't assume that management can decide on the most efficient way to utilise manpower and implement this _____. (direct)
6. Changes in utilisation are _____ to implement as they require lengthy planning. (hard)

7. Manpower utilisation is an area where management should be _____ involved. (particular)
8. _____, manpower planning is a critical area. (clear)
9. Your ideas for using the external manpower supply sound _____. (sense)
10. In any case, the risk of failure seems very _____. (real)
11. The discussion on manpower planning was extremely _____. (live)
12. _____, we will have to forecast the manpower level for next year. (eventual)

5 Word study

The following word table contains synonyms – words with the same or very similar meanings. Link each word on the left with its synonym on the right:

1. forecast	a. ensure
2. wastage	b. alter
3. necessitate	c. especially
4. vital	d. predict
5. make sure	e. utilise
6. centre around	f. stage
7. particularly	g. turnover
8. change	h. essential
9. step	i. focus on
10. use	j. require

6 Transfer

The basis of good personnel planning is to develop sound premises about the future. For this you will need three sets of forecasts:

- one for your personnel requirements
- one for the supply of outside candidates
- one for your available internal candidates

Discuss the personnel plan for your organisation or institution based on the available information.

Choose either the adjective or the adverb in each of the sentences below:

1. The first task for the interviewer is to make the candidate feel comfortable/comfortably.
2. In a panel interview the candidate may look at the interviewers nervous/nervously.
3. If the candidate sounds nervous/nervously, encourage him or her to speak on a well-known topic.
4. This approach proves clear/clearly the importance of a well-prepared strategy.
5. When the candidate appears good/well in control, it is time to move on to more probing questions.
6. If the atmosphere becomes tense/tensely, the interview leader should take charge.
7. The leader should keep the pace of the interview lively/livelily and the atmosphere friendly/friendlily.
8. In a good interview the candidate seems hard/hardly to notice the time.
9. The time for each interviewer goes very quick/quickly in a well-conducted interview.
10. Well-prepared interviewers are usually good/well at interviewing.

5 Word study

On the left are fifteen words taken from the text. On the right are synonyms for these words. Match each word on the left with its synonym.

1. structure		a.	change
2. control		b.	help
3. relevant		c.	dependable
4. assist		d.	organisation
5. objective		e.	tempo
6. assessment		f.	characteristic
7. adjust		g.	direct
8. feature		h.	finally
9. eventually		i.	exactly
10. courteous		j.	appropriate
11. reliable		k.	evaluation
12. tactic		l.	polite
13. remainder		m.	rest
14. pace		n.	aim
15. precisely		o.	strategy

6 Transfer

In the Reading passage above we looked at the effective structure and conduct of interviews from the interviewer's perspective. What advice would you give to interviewees to increase their competitive edge in interviews?

Part 2: Individual versus panel interviews

1 Warm-up

1.1 What are the advantages of individual interviews – from the organisation's, the interviewer's and the candidate's point of view?

1.2 What are the advantages of panel interviews?

2 Listening

Peter Parker, the domestic sales manager at Codix, has a vacancy in his team for a regional sales manager. This person would report to Parker and would form part of the regional sales team, consisting of three other managers. Peter has asked Sandra Morgan, the employment manager at Codix, to come along and discuss the preparations for the interview. He has also invited the three regional managers to the meeting. The meeting starts with a discussion of individual versus panel interviews. As you listen, put yourself in the position of the employment manager. You have two tasks:

- To indicate each person's preference (individual or panel)
- To get the group to decide who could act as interviewers.

Complete Chart 4.4 by putting ticks where appropriate.

Chart 4.4

| | Preference | | Interviewer |
	Individual	Panel	
Sandra Peter George Patsy Barry	—	—	

3 Comprehension/interpretation

3.1 How many candidates have been shortlisted for the post of regional sales manager?

3.2 Why is Sandra reluctant to sit in on the interview?

3.3 With what words does Peter indicate that he is prepared to change his mind?

3.4 When do they want to run the interview?

4 Language focus

4.1 Likes and preferences (see Unit 74 in *Language Reference for Business English*)

Look at the following sentences taken from the Listening passage:

'I mean, I *like* to be involved in the selection process.'
'I normally *prefer* individual interviews to panels.'
'I'*d rather* be safe than sorry.'

Now complete the following sentences with an appropriate form of the verbs given in brackets. The first one has been done for you.

1. A: John, *would you like to lead* this interview? (you like, lead)
   B: No thanks, you know I _ _ _ _ _ _ _ _ _ _ interviews – I just don't enjoy it. (not like, run)

2. This is Mary Bell. Right, Mrs Bell, _ _ _ _ _ _ _ _ _ _ ? (like, sit down)

3. A: Would you like to discuss the interview now or _ _ _ _ _ _ _ _ _ _ it later? (would rather, discuss)
   B: If possible, I _ _ _ _ _ _ _ _ _ _ each candidate immediately after their interview. (prefer, evaluate)

Now choose the best response from the choice given:

1. Right, shall we make a start?
   a. Yes, I'd like to tell you a little about my previous job.
   b. Yes, I like to tell you a little about my previous job.
   c. Yes, I'd rather to tell you a little about my previous job.

2. And what do you do in your spare time?
   a. Well, I like to ski.
   b. Well, I like skiing.
   c. Well, I like ski.

3. So, who should we ask to form the panel?
   a. First, I'd like that you ask Peter.
   b. First, I'd like you to ask Peter.
   c. First, I like you to ask Peter.

4. What about Jeremy?
   a. Well, I'd rather not ask him this time.
   b. Well, I'd rather not to ask this time.
   c. Well, I'd not rather ask him this time.

5. And Trish?
   a. Well, I'd rather you to ask her.
   b. Well, I'd rather you ask her.
   c. Well, I'd rather you asked her.

6. And the decision?
   a. I'd prefer a considered opinion to a hasty decision.
   b. I'd prefer a considered opinion than a hasty decision.
   c. I'd prefer a considered opinion more than a hasty decision.

4.2 The future with **going to** and **will** (see Units 8 and 9 in *Language Reference for Business English*)

Look at the following sentences taken from the Listening passage:

'So, the purpose of this meeting is to decide what type of interview we'*re going to hold* . . .'

'Peter is the person who *will have to* deal most frequently and closely with the new person . . .'

'I'*ll change* my position.'

Now complete the following sentences with **will** or a form of **be going to**. The first one has been done for you.

1. I hope we *will* soon find a suitable applicant for this post.
2. A: So, what are you planning to do first?
   B: Well, first we _ _ _ _ _ _ _ _ _ contact a number of recruitment agencies.
3. It is likely that three or four agencies _ _ _ _ _ _ _ _ _ be able to help.
4. We've now chosen one agency. I've contacted them to give them the brief. So, I _ _ _ _ _ _ _ _ _ contact you as soon as I've heard from them.
5. A: In fact, I'm a little worried about their fees.
   B: So, what are you going to do?
   A: First I _ _ _ _ _ _ _ _ _ discuss the fees with the MD.
6. When _ _ _ _ _ _ _ _ _ _ you _ _ _ _ _ _ _ _ _ see the MD?
7. I've arranged a meeting for this afternoon. I'm pretty sure he _ _ _ _ _ _ _ _ _ make a quick decision.
8. A: So when can you call me?
   B: I _ _ _ _ _ _ _ _ _ call you as soon as I've spoken to him.
9. If we use the same agency as last time, I know it _ _ _ _ _ _ _ _ _ be expensive.
10. In that case, leave it with me. I _ _ _ _ _ _ _ _ _ look into other possibilities, but I'm not too hopeful.

5 Word study

The ten verb phrases below are taken from the discussion. Select the correct verb from the following list to complete the expressions:

have   set   run   look   make
turn   deal   be   sit   agree

1. to _____ with the new person
2. to _____ a decision
3. to _____ a look
4. to _____ on the panel
5. to _____ up the interview
6. to _____ for a person
7. to _____ on the profile
8. to _____ into a debate
9. to _____ in on the interview
10. to _____ an interview

6 Transfer

You have been asked by your personnel director to draft a memo to your company's managers on good interview practice. Use the information from the first part of this section (together with any other points you consider important) to draft a memo. Your memo should start as follows:

FROM: Philip Bradshaw, Personnel Director
TO: Departmental Managers

GUIDELINES FOR INTERVIEWS

We have received a number of requests for interviewing support. We hope that the following guidelines will help you.

1. Consider your interview as consisting of three stages: a beginning, a middle and an end.

2. At the first stage, _____

_____

_____

_____

_____

_____

_____

_____

Finally, please feel free to contact me if you wish to discuss interviewing further.

UNIT 5
Training and development

Section A: Training

A recent report on industrial training in the UK emphasised the great need for more and better training. However, recent surveys have shown that employers are reluctant to provide it. This theme has also worried politicians for the past thirty years. So, although there is a widespread acceptance of the argument that more training needs to be provided, there is a lack of enthusiasm about making the provision. The significance of this for personnel managers is substantial. Training and development is a major feature of the personnel function, yet apathy towards training by other managers causes personnel specialists themselves to lose interest and advocate the need for training with insufficient vigour.

Part 1: Determining training needs

1 *Warm-up*

1.1 Why do you think that training suffers?

1.2 How would you justify increased investment in training within your organisation?

2 Reading

The following text deals with performance analysis – a method of analysing training needs. Performance analysis consists of ten steps:

Eliminate obstacles in system
Change the job
Cost/value analysis
Training
Reward or punishment
Performance appraisal
Practice
Set standards
Distinguish between 'can't do' and 'won't do' problems
Transfer or terminate

As you read, transfer the appropriate step name to the appropriate section in the text. Finally, complete Chart 5.1 at the end of the text.

Performance analysis basically involves verifying the fact that there is a significant performance deficiency, and then determining if that deficiency should be rectified through training or by some other means (such as changing the machinery or transferring the employee). The performance analysis procedure consists of ten steps, as shown at the end of this text.

Step 1: _____
The first step is to identify the discrepancy between present performance and target performance. In other words, if you want to improve your employee's performance, you must first determine what the person's performance is now and what you would like it to be. Examples of specific performance deficiencies are:

I expect each salesperson to make ten new contracts per week, but John averages only six.
Other plants our size average no more than two serious accidents per month, and we're averaging five.

Step 2: _____
Next determine whether rectifying the problem is worth the time and effort that you'll have to put into doing so. For example, ask, 'What is the cost of not solving the problem? Is it worth solving?' Sometimes not solving the problem is cheaper than setting up a training programme to rectify it.

Step 3: _____
This is the heart of the analysis. To distinguish between these two types of problem, ask three sets of questions:

1. Does the person know what to do, and what you expect in terms of performance?
2. Could the person do the job if he or she wanted to?
3. Does the person want to do the job, and what are the consequences of performing well?

For example, assume the problem is that you have twice the scrap you should on the number 8 assembly line. You could proceed with your analysis as follows:

1. Do the assembly workers know what is expected of them? (If not, it is a 'can't do' problem.) After speaking with the assemblers, you find that while they know they should not have more than one reject per five assemblies, they did not know that their reject rate was twice as high. You therefore suggest that a graph be placed at their work site indicating the hourly reject rate for the line.

2. Could they do the job if they wanted to? (If not, it's again a 'can't do' problem.) In other words, could the assemblers keep their rejects to one per five assemblies if they wanted to? Do they have the ability to do so? Are there any roadblocks or impediments preventing them from achieving this goal? Here you find that some problems are amenable to training. For example, several of the assemblers need to be retrained regarding the proper way to solder a joint.

3. Do they want to do their jobs? (If not, it's a 'won't do' problem.) What happens when they achieve the desired reject rate? What happens when they do not attain the desired rate? Here you find that the assemblers are never praised for minimising rejects, and in fact are never penalised for excessive rejects. You decide to solve this problem by having the supervisor on the line praise the assemblers each hour if the desired reject rate is attained or to express some displeasure when the rate is exceeded.

This analysis therefore identified several problems, only one of which required retraining. In this case it's possible that just the graph (which shows the assemblers how they are doing) and the supervisor's praise (which reinforces their good performance) may be sufficient to inexpensively rectify the problem, without the expense of retraining any assemblers. Once you identify the problem as either a 'can't do' or a 'won't do' problem, you can proceed as follows:

Step 4: _____

Sometimes, as in our example, employees don't perform up to par because they don't know what par is, or because they think they are already performing at the required standard. In this step, therefore, review your performance standards and your employees' understanding of what they are expected to do. Also determine if they know that they are not performing up to par.

Step 5: ————————————————————————————————

Ask, for instance, 'Does the material arrive at this person's work station on time?' Sometimes an easy solution is to provide a job aid. For example, one firm found that its electronic assemblers were having trouble remembering which wire was to be soldered to which junction. The job aid in this case involved colour coding all wires and junctions. The assemblers can now see at a glance which wire goes where.

Step 6: ————————————————————————————————

Sometimes employees lose a skill or knowledge because they haven't had the opportunity or the need to use it. Hotel fire drills are an example of ensuring that employees maintain satisfactory skill and knowledge levels.

Step 7: ————————————————————————————————

As we have seen, this is not always the best solution; in fact, it can sometimes be the most expensive one. However, if this is the root of the problem, then you need to ensure that you set your objectives, provide the training, and then evaluate it.

Step 8: ————————————————————————————————

Sometimes this is the best way to handle 'can't do' problems. For example, most sales jobs consist of three parts: prospecting, demonstrating, and closing. Training someone who is good at prospecting and demonstrating also to close a deal is often difficult. On the other hand, some hot-shot closers are best-off if they don't waste their time prospecting and demonstrating. The solution here is to change the sales job by subdividing it and have one person prospect and demonstrate, and another close.

Step 9: ————————————————————————————————

Finally, if after all your efforts, the person wants to do the job, but can't, then this may be the appropriate and necessary course of action.

Step 10: ————————————————————————————————

Often, it's not a 'can't do', but a 'won't do' problem: the employee could do the job if he or she wanted to. Here you have a motivation problem and must decide what rewards or punishments are appropriate. For our assemblers, for instance, the supervisor's praise may be enough of a reward to keep the assemblers' reject rates to a minimum.

Chart 5.1 Perfomance analysis

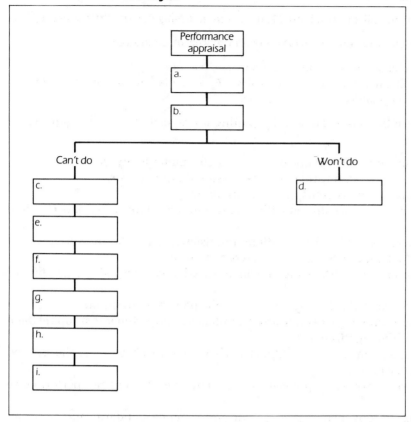

3 Comprehension/interpretation

3.1 What is performance discrepancy?
3.2 What is the heart of the analysis?
3.3 If all your efforts to solve a 'can't do' problem fail, what may be your only course of action?
3.4 What is at the root of 'won't do' problems?

4 Language focus

4.1 Verb + preposition (see Unit 31 in *Language Reference for Business English*)

Look at the following sentences taken from the Reading passage:

> 'The performance analysis procedure *consists of* ten steps . . .'
> 'Here you find that the assemblers are never *praised for* minimising rejects, and in fact are never *penalised for* excessive rejects.'

Complete the following sentences by putting a preposition into the gap, where necessary:

1. At the moment we are involved _____ performance analysis.
2. We hope _____ an improvement as a result of this analysis.
3. Next we are going to discuss _____ our findings.
4. By looking _____ a solution with a team of representatives, we expect to find one.
5. At this stage we need to ask questions and listen _____ the answers.
6. We have to distinguish _____ two types of problem.
7. The first question is: 'Does the person know what is expected _____ him or her?
8. The way to check this is to speak _____ the person in question.
9. The next question is: 'Are there any roadblocks or impediments stopping them _____ achieving this goal?
10. Another question is: 'What happens when they reach _____ the desired performance rate?'
11. Often workers are never praised _____ achieving the desired performance rate.
12. Remember to look again _____ your performance standards and your employees' understanding of what they are expected to do.
13. Ask _____ your employees if their material arrives at their work stations on time.
14. Job aid can often help _____ problems.

4.2 Verb . . . *ing* (see Unit 12 in *Language Reference for Business English*)

Look at the following sentences taken from the Reading passage:

> 'The solution here is to change the sales job by *subdividing* it.'
> 'They don't waste their time *prospecting* and *demonstrating*.'
> 'One firm found that its electronic assemblers were having trouble *remembering* which wire was to be soldered to which junction.'
> 'Is it worth *solving*?'

Complete the following sentences with a verb . . . *ing* construction. You need either to rewrite the italicised part or to combine the sentences given to form a new sentence, as shown in the examples.

1. Performance analysis involves *an investigation of* the performance of a company's workforce.
   Performance analysis involves investigating the performance of a company's workforce.
2. We identified performance deficiency. This was not difficult.
   We had no difficulty identifying performance deficiency.
3. There are other methods *through which we can rectify* deficiences.
4. You should consider other possibilities. One example is to change the machinery.
5. Identify the discrepancy between present performance and target performance. You should start with this.
6. First determine what the person's present performance is. It is worth it.
7. But perhaps the cost *of a solution to the problem* is out of proportion to the benefits.
8. Sometimes it is cheaper not to solve a problem than *if we invest* in a training programme.
   Sometimes, not solving . . .
9. You can distinguish between different types of deficiency problem *if you ask* three sets of questions.
10. Perhaps the worker doesn't understand what is expected. He has trouble with it.
11. *While you are speaking* with a worker, you may find out that he or she doesn't know the extent of the deficiencies.
12. They might suggest *that they take* some simple steps to improve performance.
13. Sometimes workers have to wait for materials at their work stations. They waste time.
14. So you often remedy deficiencies without major expenditure. You can look forward to it.

5 Word study

The words on the left are taken from the text. On the right is a list of synonyms. Link each word on the left with its synonym on the right.

1. significant	a. differentiate
2. verify	b. help
3. deficiency	c. important
4. rectify	d. required standard
5. discrepancy	e. check
6. distinguish	f. difference/gap
7. attain	g. failure
8. inexpensively	h. take away
9. par	i. correct
10. eliminate	j. cheaply
11. aid	k. deal with
12. handle	l. reach

6 Transfer

You are the supervisor of a group of workers at Codix whose job is to mix the ingredients for one of their product lines (sweets). You find that the quality is not what it should be, and that many of the batches are rejected. Your own boss tells you that you'd better start improving the training of your workers.

Discuss how would you go about assessing whether it is in fact a training problem.

Part 2: Setting up an induction programme

1 Warm-up

1.1 How do new employees usually feel on their first day?
1.2 What then are the objectives of induction or orientation programmes?

2 Listening

New employees are most likely to leave an organisation in the early weeks of employment: a period often described as the induction crisis before the period of settled connection begins.

Codix are introducing a new initiative at departmental level to integrate new employees into the organisation. In this extract from a workshop you will hear Sandra Morgan, the employment manager at Codix, together with some of the company's supervisors and department heads. As you listen, complete Chart 5.2, which lists the steps for the company's induction programme.

Chart 5.2   Induction programme

ITEMS TO BE DISCUSSED BY DEPARTMENT HEAD OR SUPERVISOR
WITH NEW EMPLOYEE

First day of employment
1. Introduction to fellow workers
2. Information on:
    - The toilets and washrooms
    - The coffee machine
    - Lunch
    - The notice-board

Rules and policies
1. Hours:

    - _____
    - _____
    - _____
    - _____

2. Pay:

    - _____
    - _____
    - How paid

3. _____
4. _____
5. _____

    - _____
    - When to inform
    - _____

6. _____
7. Basic rules:

    - _____
    - _____
    - _____

---

3 Comprehension/interpretation

3.1 What does Mary call the system of working time at Codix?
    What is the time called when everyone must be at work?
3.2 What's the maximum amount of overtime per month that can be claimed?
3.3 How does Codix pay its secretaries?
3.4 How long can a secretary be away from work sick before a sick note is required?

4 Language focus

4.1 Modals of ability, possibility and necessity (see Units 18 and 19 in *Language Reference for Building English*)

Look at the following sentences taken from the Listening passage:

'That's the maximum that *can* be claimed.'
'We *can't* pay you.'
'Ten of these eighteen days *must* be taken during July when we are closed.'
'You *mustn't* have more than 10 hours' overtime.'

Rewrite the following sentences using an appropriate modal verb. The first one has been done for you.

1. The flexitime system enables you to choose your start and finish time.
   With the flexitime system you can choose your start and finish time.
2. The flexitime system requires you all to be here from 10 till 3.
3. You are required not to put in more than 41 hours per week.
4. The flexitime system allows you to claim for an extra 2½ hours per week.
5. In the past, company regulations allowed you to claim 8 hours' overtime pay per month.
6. In the past, company regulations also required you to get authorisation for overtime.
7. Now company regulations do not require you to get authorisation for overtime.
8. Under no circumstances is it possible for us to provide an advance on salary.
9. Company regulations do not permit us to take all our holiday entitlement in summer.
10. If you fall ill, it is not necessary for you to supply a sick note during the first seven days of absence.

4.2 **Some, any** and related words (see Unit 58 in *Language Reference for Business English*)

Look at the following sentences taken from the Listening passage:

'But what I'd like to do now is listen to *some* little presentations . . .'
'Right, are there *any* questions about pay?'
'And if we don't have *any* cover, it's hard for the others who have to take over your work.'
'Of course, there's always *someone* who hasn't got *any* money . . .'

Complete the following sentences with **some**, **any** or a related word:

1. First I'd like to give you _ _ _ _ _ _ _ _ _ _ information about the toilets and washrooms.
2. If _ _ _ _ _ _ _ _ _ _ wants to put _ _ _ _ _ _ _ _ _ _ up on the notice board, please feel free.
3. This is a short presentation that I _ _ _ _ _ _ _ _ _ _ give to the new secretaries.
4. That sounds fine. Do you _ _ _ _ _ _ _ _ _ _ talk about the social side?
5. That question seems _ _ _ _ _ _ _ _ _ _ complex. Do you mind if I take it at the end of this session?
6. Right. Are there _ _ _ _ _ _ _ _ _ _ more questions?
7. Well, have you seen my notes? I can't find them _ _ _ _ _ _ _ _ _ _ .
8. First of all I'd like to tell you all _ _ _ _ _ _ _ _ _ _ about the rules and regulations here.
9. You may be wondering why we need rules _ _ _ _ _ _ _ _ _ _ .
10. You need to decide _ _ _ _ _ _ _ _ _ _ before next Monday if you want to work the early shift or the late shift.
11. I don't think I've got _ _ _ _ _ _ _ _ _ _ else to say.
12. If there is anything _ _ _ _ _ _ _ _ _ _ you want to ask, now is the time.

5 Word study

Put the following words into four groups so that words from similar areas are together.

sickness	overtime	organisation	chat
department	absence	flexitime	section
presentation	division	pep talk	core time
starting time	introduction	illness	sick note

6 Transfer

Design a 90-minute induction programme for production workers joining Codix, listing the items that you would cover in terms of:

- general company orientation, and
- specific department orientation.

Section B: Development

Management development is any attempt to improve current or future managerial performance by imparting knowledge, changing attitudes, or increasing skills. Different levels of management have different development needs. For example, supervisory and middle management are likely to stress technical skills such as evaluating and appraising employees, setting objectives, communicating and disciplining. At the executive level, development needs are likely to stress general business skills like financial management, budgeting and labour relations as well as OD (organisational development) skills such as managing time and team building.

Management development techniques can be broadly divided into:

- on-the-job training, and
- off-the-job training.

Part 1: On-the-job training methods

1 Warm-up

1.1 In what ways is management development broader than training?
1.2 What is the relationship between management development and organisation development?

2 Reading

From the information given and your own interpretation of the text, complete Chart 5.3 at the end of the text.

MANAGERIAL ON-THE-JOB TRAINING

On-the-job training is one of the most popular development methods. Important techniques here include job rotation, coaching, junior boards and understudy assignments.

JOB ROTATION

With job rotation you move management trainees from department to department to broaden their understanding of all phases of the business. The trainee – often a recent college or university graduate – may spend several months in each department; this not only helps broaden his or her experience, but also helps the person discover the jobs he or she prefers. The person may just be an observer in each department, but more commonly gets fully involved in its operations; he or she thus learns the department's business by actually doing it, whether it involves sales, production, finance or some other function.

Job rotation has several other advantages. In addition to providing a well-rounded training experience for each person, it helps avoid stagnation through the constant introduction of new points of view in each department. And, it tests the trainee and helps identify the person's strong and weak points.

Rotation does have disadvantages. It encourages 'generalisation' and tends to be more appropriate for developing general line managers than functional staff experts, You also have to be careful not to inadvertently forget a trainee at some deserted outpost.

COACHING/UNDERSTUDY APPROACH

The coaching/understudy approach is particularly useful for junior-management training. In this approach, the trainee works directly with the person he or she is to replace; the latter is in turn responsible for the trainee's coaching. Normally, the understudy relieves the executive of certain responsibilities, thereby giving the trainee a chance to perform an increasing range of management tasks and gradually learn the job. The coach works to improve the trainee's performance by discussion, exhortation, encouragement and understanding. It is therefore vital that the coach is someone who has experienced those things which the trainee is now learning. This approach helps ensure that the employer will have trained managers to assume key positions when they're vacated due to retirement, promotions, transfers, or terminations. And it helps guarantee the long-run development of company-bred top managers.

JUNIOR BOARDS

Unlike job rotation (which aims to familiarise the trainees with the problems of each department), junior boards aim to give promising young middle managers experience in analysing overall company problems. The idea of a junior board (also sometimes called multiple management) is to give trainees top-level analysis and policy-making experience by having 10 to 12 of them sit on a 'junior' board of directors. The members of such committees come from various departments and make recommendations regarding top-level issues like organisation structure, executive compensation, and interdepartmental conflict to the official board of directors. It thus provides middle-management trainees with on-the-job training and experience in dealing with organisation-wide problems.

ACTION LEARNING

Action learning involves giving middle-management trainees released time to work full time on projects, analysing and solving problems in departments other than their own. The trainees meet periodically with a four- or five-person project group where their findings and progress are discussed and debated. Action learning is similar to junior boards except that trainees generally work full time on their projects, rather than analysing a problem as a committee as they would on junior boards.

The idea of developing managers this way has pros and cons. It gives trainees real experience with actual problems, and to that extent can develop skills like problem analysis and planning. Furthermore, the trainees (working with the others in the group) can and do find solutions to major problems. The main drawback is that in releasing trainees to work on outside projects, the employer loses, in a sense, the full-time services of a competent manager, while the trainee often finds it hard to return to his or her old position (which is usually filled by a stand-in manager).

MENTORING

Mentoring is similar to coaching in that it is based on a coaching/understudy relationship, though the protégé is chosen with especial attention to social background as well as professional skill. Mentoring is seen as offering a wide range of advantages for the development of the protégé, coaching as described above being just one of the benefits of the relationship. Kram (1983) identifies two broad functions of mentoring; first, career functions which are those aspects of the relationship that primarily enhance career development; secondly, psychosocial functions which are those aspects of the relationship that primarily enhance a sense of competence, clarity of identity and effectiveness in the managerial role. In mentoring there is a much greater stress on career success than in coaching, and individuals are selected for mentoring, because amongst other things, they are good performers, from the right social background, and know the potential mentors socially. There are advantages in the relationship for mentors as well as protégés – these include reflected glory from a successful protégé, the development of supporters throughout the organisation, and the facilitation of their own promotion by adequate training of a replacement.

PEER RELATIONSHIPS

Although mentor–protégé relationships have been shown to be related to high levels of career success, not all developing managers have access to such a relationship. Supportive peer relationships at work are potentially more available to the individual and offer a number of benefits for the development of both individuals. The benefits that are available depend on the nature of the peer relationship, and Kram and Isabella (1985) have identified three groups of peer relationships which are differentiated by their primary development functions. Information peers provide primarily an opportuntiy for information sharing; collegial peers share career-strategising, job-related feedback and friendship; special peers provide reciprocal confirmation, emotional support, personal feedback and friendship. Most of us benefit from one or a number of peer relationships at work but often we do not readily appreciate their contribution towards our development.

Chart 5.3 Summary table of on-the-job management training approaches

Training approach	Suitable for	Objectives
1. Job rotation	_____ _____	1. Helps broaden the person's experience 2. _____ _____ _____
2. Coaching/ understudy	_____ _____	1. Gives the trainee a chance to perform an increasing range of management tasks and gradually learn the job 2. _____ _____ _____ _____
3. Junior boards	_____ _____	1. _____ _____ _____ _____ 2. Give trainees top-level analysis and policy-making experience
4. Action learning	_____ _____	1. _____ _____ _____ 2. Develops skills like problem analysis and planning
5. Mentoring	Junior and middle management	1. _____ _____ 2. Enhances a sense of competence, clarity of identity and effectiveness in the managerial role

3 Comprehension/interpretation

3.1   What type of manager is job rotation more appropriate for developing?

3.2   What methods does the coach use in the coach/understudy approach to improve the understudy's performance?

3.3   What two drawbacks of action learning are mentioned in the text?

3.4   What three types of peers are mentioned in the text?

4 Language focus

4.1   Relative clauses (see Unit 39 in *Language Reference for Business English*)

Look at the following sentences taken from the Reading passage:

> 'It is therefore vital that the coach is someone *who has experienced those things which the trainee is now learning*.'
> 'The benefits *that are available* depend on the nature of the peer relationship.'
> 'The trainees meet periodically with a four- or five-person project group, *where their findings and progress are discussed and debated*.'

Now combine the following sentences using a relative clause. You may need to make some small changes to the words and the word order to make your final sentence sound more natural.

1. On-the-job training is one of the most popular development methods. On-the-job training includes job rotation, coaching, junior boards, and understudy assignments.
2. Job trainees spend time in each department. There they broaden their experience.
3. The trainee becomes involved in the business. He or she learns more about its activities.
4. Job rotation has several advantages. The most important advantage is that it provides a well-rounded training experience for each person.
5. The coaching/understudy approach is particularly useful for junior management trainees. They will work directly under the person. They will replace that person.
6. This approach helps ensure that the employer will have trained managers in the future. Then the posts will need to be filled.
7. Junior boards of directors are composed of promising young middle managers. The members of such boards come from various departments.
8. The protégés are chosen. They must be good performers and come from the right social background.
9. Peer relationships are very common. These can provide a number of benefits for the development of both individuals.

4.2   Comparing and contrasting ideas (see Unit 72 in *Language Reference for Business English*)

Look at the following sentences taken from the Reading passage:

> '*Although mentor–protégé relationships have been shown to be related to high levels of career success*, not all developing managers have access to such a relationship.'
> 'The employer loses, in a sense, the full-time services of a competent manager, *while the trainee often finds it hard to return to his or her old position.*'
> 'Most of us benefit from one or a number of peer relationships at work *but often we do not readily appreciate their contribution towards our development.*'

Now rewrite the following sentences using the language or construction given in brackets. The first one has been done for you.

1. Both managers and non-managers may receive training. However, the types of training programme are likely to differ. (clause of contrast)
    Both managers and non-managers may receive training, (al)though/but the types of training programme are likely to differ.
2. Non-managers are likely to receive technical training for their present job; managers are likely to receive assistance in developing skills for future jobs. (clause of contrast)
3. Although it is easy to offer training programmes, it is more difficult to change behaviour. (sentence connector)
4. Training programmes improve knowledge, but do not necessarily improve effectiveness. (phrase of contrast)
5. Off-the-job training takes place outside the actual workplace while on-the-job training takes place in it. (in contrast)
6. On-the-job training focuses on workplace skills. However, it is also likely to include classroom instruction. (phrase of contrast)
7. Although role playing can be an enjoyable and inexpensive way to develop many new skills, some trainees feel that it is childish. (sentence connector)
8. On-the-job experience is by far the most popular form of management development. However, the preferred techniques differ according to organisational level. (clause of contrast)

5 Word study

Noun + noun compounds are common in English. The compound *university graduate* means 'graduate from a university'; the compound *employee turnover* means 'turnover of employees'. Notice that, in forming the compound, the first noun is typically put in the singular (employee) rather than left in the plural (employees). What are the noun compounds for the following:

1. the rotation of jobs
2. a member of staff who is an expert
3. the development of one's career
4. a person who is training to become a manager
5. a method for developing something
6. the problems of the company
7. compensation for executives
8. learning through action
9. the analysis of problems
10. peers with whom one shares information

6 Transfer

Each of you is to play one of the senior management team at Codix – with one of you acting as the personnel director. As you know, the company has been going through a tough period with a significant slow down of sales. The personnel director believes that one of the ways to boost the company's morale is to set up some additional mangement training programmes. However, the personnel director thinks that the other members of the senior management team will be against the idea.

The personnel director should:

- present the ideas,
- suggest where management training could be effective, and
- outline some approaches to different types of management training.

The other members of the meeting should respond according to their belief about the value and appropriacy of the personnel director's ideas.

Part 2: Reviewing the development needs

1 Warm-up

1.1 What communication skills are important for junior managers?
1.2 Why are case studies and role plays important off-the-job training approaches?

2 Listening

Codix has now appointed a training and development manager, Dianne O'Connor, who reports to Philip Bradshaw, the personnel director. Her first task is to review the development needs of the junior managers in the organisation. As an initial step, in order to collect information, she has sent round a questionnaire asking the junior managers to tick those areas in which they feel they need further development. One manager still hasn't returned his questionnaire, so Dianne phones his office.

As you listen, complete Chart 5.4.

Chart 5.4   Questionnaire

TO: Junior managers
FROM: Dianne O'Connor, training and development manager

Please indicate your needs by ticking the appropriate box and return to me not later than Wednesday, 22 April.
Name: John Graham

Position: _____

Development needs   **Priority**

                                                High   Medium   Low

1. Motivating others
2. Evaluation and appraisal
3. Leadership
4. Oral communication
5. Understanding human behaviour
6. Developing and training subordinates
7. Setting objectives and priorities
8. Written communication
9. Selecting employees

3 Comprehension/interpretation

3.1   Why has John Graham gone down to the Hoverton plant?
3.2   Why does Dianne want to get all the responses?
3.3   What is the problem at the Hoverton plant?
3.4   What does Dianne have to do after she has got John Graham's responses?

4 Language focus

4.1 Telephoning (see Skill 3 in *Language Reference for Business English*)

Look at the following extracts taken from the Listening passage:

> *'This is Dianne O'Connor from the training department here. Could I speak to John Graham please?'*
> *'I'm just phoning to. . . .'*
> *'Sorry for causing the inconvenience.'*

The sentences in each of the following telephone conversations have been mixed up. You have to put the sentences in the correct order. The first sentence is shown.

CONVERSATION 1
(Ring, ring)
B: Oh, I see.
A: Yes, it's 1076.
B: Yes, certainly.
B: No, I'm afraid not. Can I take a message?
A: Bye.
B: Hello, this is Alan Clark from the training department here. Could I speak to John Graham please?
A: Right, thanks.
B: Right. Bye.
A: Yes please. Could you ask him to phone me when he gets back?
A: I'm sorry, John's in a meeting at the moment.
B: By the way, could you give me your extension?
A: D'you know when he'll be back in the office?
A: Ann Gordon. *(1)*

CONVERSATION 2

(Ring, ring)

B: Do I need to contact them myself?

B: Yes, that's right.

B: Well, it's about the training course.

B: Alan Clark. *(1)*

A: Bye for now.

A: The training centre need to know when you can attend.

A: Hello, Alan. John Graham here.

A: Fine thanks. Alan, I'm just returning your call.

B: Let me see. I've put down week 43.

B: Bye.

B: Oh, hello John. How are you?

A: So, what can I do for you?

B: Right, John, that's all I wanted to know.

A: You mean the French one?

A: Fine. I'll give them the information.

B: Yes, thanks.

A: No, they'll be in touch with you.

5 Word study

Verb + preposition constructions are common in English – especially in spoken English. Here are some verb phrases. Match those on the left with an expression on the right which has the same meaning.

1. sort out	a. omit
2. be back	b. wait
3. be through	c. solve
4. hang on	d. reach
5. put down	e. return
6. miss out	f. be broken
7. be down	g. be connected
8. get through to	h. write

6 Transfer

1. As training and development manager design a development questionnaire for junior managers in your organisation.

2. Circulate it to your junior managers for them to fill in according to their needs.

3. Call one of the junior managers to get and write down his/her responses.

UNIT 6
Compensation, incentives and benefits

Section A: Pay

A strange thing about payment is that managers seem to shy away from actually using the word. We hear about compensation, reward or remuneration, yet the first two do not mean payment. Remuneration does mean the same as payment but has five more letters and is often misspelt. Payment seems to us a good, solid, clear word to encompass everything from basic rates to pensions.

Part 1: What the employee expects from the payment contract

1 Warm-up

1.1 Why are compensation and reward not the same as payment?
1.2 What is the difference between wages and salaries?

2 Reading

As you read choose the appropriate title for each objective from the following list.

Rights
Composition
'Felt fair'
Purchasing power
Relativities

Also use the information in the final paragraph to complete Chart 6.1 about employee payment preferences by putting a tick (✓) or a cross (✗) in the boxes indicated.

WHAT THE EMPLOYEE EXPECTS FROM THE PAYMENT CONTRACT

Those who are paid, and those who administer payment schemes have objectives for the payment contract which differ according to whether one is the recipient or the administrator of the payments. The contract for payment will be satisfactory in so far as it meets the objectives of the parties. Therefore we can consider the range of objectives, starting with employees.

First objective: _____

The absolute level of weekly or monthly earnings determines the recipient's standard of living, and will therefore be the most important consideration for most employees. How much can I buy? Employees are rarely satisfied about their purchasing power, and the annual pay adjustment will do little more than reduce dissatisfaction. The two main reasons for this are inflation and rising expectations.

Second objective: _____

Elliott Jacques (1962) claimed that every employee had a strong feeling about the level of payment that was reasonable for the job. Here we move away from the absolute level or earnings to the first of a series of aspects of relative income. In most cases this will be a very rough, personalised evaluation of what is seen as appropriate.

The employee who feels underpaid is likely to demonstrate the conventional symptoms of withdrawal from the job: looking for another, carelessness, disgruntlement, lateness, absence and the like. If he feels that he is overpaid, he may simply feel dishonest, or may seek to justify his existence in some way, like trying to look busy, that is not necessarily productive.

Third objective: _____

This concerns a different aspect of relative income. It is linked to the notion of entitlement to a particular share of the company's profits or the nation's wealth. The employee is here thinking about whether the division of earnings is providing fair shares of the Gross National Product. 'To each according to his needs' is overlaid on 'a fair day's pay . . .' This is a strong feature of most trade union arguments and part of the general preoccupation with individual's rights. Mainly this is the long-standing debate about who should enjoy the fruits of labour.

Fourth objective: _____

'How much do I (or we) get compared to . . . group X?' This is a slightly different version of the equitable argument. It is not the question of whether the employee feels the remuneration to be reasonable in relation to the job that he does, but in relation to the jobs that other people do.

There are many potential comparators, and the basis of comparison can alter. The Pay Board (1974) pointed out three. First is the definition of pay. Is it basic rates or is it earnings? Over how long is the pay compared? Many groups have a level of payment that varies from one time of the year to another. Second is the method of measuring changes; absolute amount of money or percentage: £5 is 10 per cent of £50 but 5 per cent of £100. Third is the choice of pay dates. Nearly all employees receive annual adjustments to their pay, but not all at the same time, and the period between settlements can be crucial to perceived relativities.

Fifth objective: _____

How is the pay package made up? The growing complexity and sophistication of payment arrangements raises all sorts of questions. Is £200 pay for sixty hours' work better than £140 for forty hours' work? The arithmetical answer that the rate per hour for the forty hour arrangement is marginally better than for sixty hours is only part of the argument. The other aspects will relate to the individual, his circumstances and the conventions of his working group and reference groups. Another question might be: Is £140 per week, plus a pension, better than £160 per week without? Such questions do not produce universally applicable answers because they can be quantified to such a limited extent, but some kernels can be suggested as generalisations:

1. Younger workers are more interested in high direct earnings at the expense of indirect benefits, like pensions and sick pay, which will be of more interest to older workers. In addition older workers will, of course, still be interested in basic pay.

2. Incentive payment arrangements are likely to interest employees who either see a reliable prospect of enhancing earnings through the ability to control their own activities, or who see the incentive scheme as an opportunity to wrest control of their personal activities (which provide little intrinsic satisfaction) away from management by regulating their earnings.

3. Married women are seldom interested in payment arrangements that depend on overtime.

4. Overtime is used by many men to produce an acceptable level of purchasing power; particularly among the lower-paid. This group will thus be less interested in benefits.

5. Pensions and sickness payment arrangements beyond statutory minima are a *sine qua non* of white-collar employment, and are of growing importance in manual employment.

Chart 6.1   Employee payment preferences

	Basic rate	Overtime	Incentives	Benefits
Younger workers	☐	☐	☐	☐
Older workers	☐	O	O	☐
The low paid	☐	☐	O	☐
Married women	☐	☐	O	O
Long-term employees	O	O	☐	O
White-collar employees	O	O	O	☐

3   Comprehension/interpretation

3.1   What are the two main reasons that employees are generally dissatisfied with their purchasing power?

3.2   Give five examples of how a worker will probably show that he feels he is underpaid.

3.3   What strong trade union argument or principle in relation to pay is mentioned in the text?

3.4   What three boxes can an employee use to compare his/her pay with that of others?

4   Language focus

4.1   Genitive forms (see Unit 47 in *Language Reference for Business English*)

Look at the following genitive phrases taken from the Reading passage:

'the *recipient's* the standard of living'
'the *company's* profits or the *nation's* wealth'
'Is £200 pay for sixty *hours'* work better than £140 for forty *hours'* work?'
'the conventions *of* his working group'

Now combine the following nouns by using a genitive form. The first one has been done for you.

1. the results – last year   *last year's results*
2. the beginning – last week
3. the resignation – the chairman
4. the debts – the departments
5. the improvement – our trading position
6. the economic prospects – the regions
7. the agenda – the meeting – today
8. the targets – the division
9. the effect – the late delivery
10. the decision – the banks

4.2 Each, every and all (see Unit 61 in *Language Reference for Business English*)

Look at the following extracts taken from the Reading passage:

'To *each* according to his needs . . .'
'Elliott Jacques (1962) claimed that *every* employee had a strong feeling . . . ?
'The growing complexity and sophistication of payment arrangements raises *all* sorts of questions?

Are the following sentences right or wrong? If wrong, make the necessary correction.

1. We have checked each equipment.
2. We have now checked every of the contracts.
3. All the works in the factory are reviewed annually.
4. We provide a fair day's pay for all.
5. All people in the organisation have a pay review every year.

Now complete the following sentences with **all, each, every** or a compound:

1. We have done _____ possible to try to improve working conditions.
2. We review the pay of _____ of the workers once a year.
3. _____ twelve months we appraise the performance of our employees.
4. He has a bad record of service _____ where he has worked.
5. _____ time that pay bargaining starts, productivity goes down.

5 Word study

The following exercise is based on words taken from the text. On the left are verbs and on the right nouns. Complete the table.

Verbs	Nouns
pay	_____
_____	recipient/reception
satisfy	_____
earn	_____
_____	consideration
adjust	_____
reduce	_____
_____	expectation
_____	evaluation
withdraw	_____
exist	_____
entitle	_____
_____	division
_____	argument
enjoy	_____
_____	comparison/comparator
vary	_____
choose	_____
_____	arrangement
_____	difference

6 Transfer

Your employer has offered you a remuneration package consisting of any of the items opposite, as long as the total is not more than X. What proportion of each item would you choose?

Bonus	Profit allocation			Variable elements – Irregular – Variable amounts – Usually discretionary	
	Discretionary sum				
Incentive	Group calculation basis				
	Individual calculation basis				
Overtime payment					
Premia	Occasional				
	Contractual				
Benefits	Fringe benefits			Fixed elements – Regular – Rarely variable – Usually contractual	
	Payment in kind	Other			
		Accommodation			
		Car			
	Benefit schemes	Other			
		Pension			
		Sick pay			
Basic rate of payment				Basic	

The total potential pay package

Discuss your choices as:

- production line workers
- junior managers

Then one person in each group should make a presentation to another group outlining the demands/requests for their group.

Part 2: What the employer expects from the payment contract

1 Warm-up

1.1 If we imagine that basic rates of pay are at one end of the payment spectrum and pensions at the other, what other aspects of payment are there in between?

1.2 In your country do you have waged and salaried employees? If so, in which category do the following fail?

Manual unskilled
Semi-skilled
Clerical/secretarial
Supervisory

2 Listening

Philip Bradshaw, the personnel director of Codix, a leading producer of confectionery in the UK, is a member of the Association of Personnel Managers (APM). This professional organisation holds both national and local meetings for personnel specialists. These meetings are of different types – some are round table discussions, some presentations, and some formal dinners with guest speakers. Philip is the chairman of the northern branch. This evening there is a presentation entitled 'The contract for payment – the employer's objectives', and Philip is going to introduce the speaker and the subject.

You are a member of the audience. As you listen, complete Chart 6.2 about the employer's objectives.

Chart 6.2 The contract for payment – the employer's objectives

Objectives	Basis
1. _____	1. Pride
	2. Elimination of a variable from the _____
	_____
2. _____	1. Paying what is sufficiently competitive to attract and keep:
	• _____
	• _____
3. _____	1. _____, e.g. piecework
	2. _____
4. Motivation and _____	1. _____
5. _____	1. The significance of employment costs in the organisation

3 Comprehension/interpretation

3.1 According to the speaker, what reputation do low-paying firms have?

3.2 Which three control methods are no longer so readily available or effective for employers?

3.3 What does the speaker believe about the relationship between incentive payment schemes and productivity?

3.4 What three expectations do workers have about their pay?

4 Language focus

4.1   Cause and effect (see Unit 77 in *Language Reference for Business English*)

Look at the following sentences taken from the Listening passage:

'I *know* that we won't lose a good guy *because* the money isn't right.'
'It's *because of* the money.'
'But in recent times this has become difficult *due to* the unwillingness of most employees to see their pay fluctuate wildly.'

Now rewrite the following sentences using the construction given in brackets and making any other necessary grammatical, word order or stylistic changes. The first one has been done for you.

1. They want to work for us because we pay well. (sentence connector)
    We pay well. So, they want to work for us.
2. We pay well because it gives us prestige. (phrase of cause)
3. We feel proud to be good payers because of the knowledge that we are doing something better than others. (clause of cause)
4. Then if workers leave they can't say it's because the pay is low. (verb or cause)
    Workers can't say . . .
5. Our competitors can't attract the quality of worker that we can because they pay poorly. (sentence connector)
6. We base our payment on piecework because it is simple to administer. (phrase of clause)
7. Piecework can lead to fluctuations in pay packets. (verb of effect)
8. Employees effectively control overtime because they use it more extensively than the employers. (sentence connector)
9. The pool of women as a reservoir of inexpensive, temporary labour has decreased substantially; so employers have lost this cheap source of labour. (verb of cause)
    The decrease of . . .
10. It is simplistic to assume that worker motivation and productivity will rise because of increased payments. (clause of cause)

4.2   Increase and decrease (see Unit 68 in *Language Reference for Business English*)

Look at the following sentences taken from the Listening passage:

'I *raise* the rates of all my boys by 20 per cent over that.'
'If payments *rise*, so will motivation and productivity.'
'There may be many ways of organising the pay packet that will . . . *reduce* payment costs.'
'The pool of women as a reservoir of inexpensive, temporary labour has *decreased* substantially . . .'

Now rewrite the following sentences using the construction shown and making any other necessary changes. The first one has been done for you.

1. Firstly it is 'a good thing' if we can make a slight increase in our payments. (transitive verb)
   Firstly it is 'a good thing' if we can increase our payments slightly.
2. If our rates go up, then we have taken money out of the equation. (transitive verb)
3. If a company decreases its rates, then it will certainly get the reputation of being a poor employer. (noun)
4. If we want to recruit suitably qualified staff, we mustn't have a further fall in rates. (transitive verb)
5. We mustn't have a cut in control of payment operations. (transitive verb)
6. In fact we must reduce payment costs. (noun)
7. Piecework can cause dramatic increases and decreases of pay. (intransitive verbs)
8. The costs of redundancy, short-term lay-offs and dismissals have risen sharply. (noun)
9. It is important in our industry that employment costs remain stable. (transitive verb)
10. Employees have expectations of pay rises. (intransitive verb)

5 Word study

The following list of words contains four nouns, four verbs, four adjectives and four adverbs. First identify the part of speech of each word and write *N* (noun), *V* (verb), *Adj* (adjective) or *Adv* (adverb) next to it. Then link each word to its synonym or definition on the right.

1. competition	a. rise and fall wildly
2. withhold	b. change
3. facilitate	c. skilled
4. potentially	d. enable
5. pride	e. widely
6. rational	f. enough
7. volume	g. struggle to gain advantage
8. experienced	h. reasonable
9. vary	i. high opinion of oneself
10. reputation	j. keep back on purpose
11. fluctuate	k. opinion held by others
12. sufficiently	l. quantity
13. extensively	m. trained
14. qualified	n. traditional
15. conventional	o. appropriately
16. suitably	p. possibly

6 Transfer

As employee relations manager at Codix you have just received a demand for a wage rise of 10.5 per cent from the workers. Their wage rise last year was 7.5 per cent; inflation is running at 8 per cent; other companies in your region are offering 9 per cent.

Write a letter to the union leader in Codix explaining the comany's view on wage rises and give reasons for turning down the union's pay demand.

Section B: Incentives and benefits

Incentive payments remain one of the ideas that fascinate managers as they search for the magic formula. Somewhere there is a method of linking payment and per- formance so effectively that their movements will coincide, enabling the manager to leave the workers on 'automatic', while s/he can attend to more important matters such as strategic planning or going to lunch. This conviction has sustained a continuing search for this elusive formula. However, incentive plans do not only apply to workers, and there are a number of ways to categorise them. For simplicity we will use the following categorisation: incentives for production workers; incentives for managers and executives; incentives for salespeople; merit pay as an incentive (primarily for white-collar and professional employees); and organisation-wide incentives.

Part 1: Developing effective incentive plans

1 Warm-up

1.1 Why do companies offer financial incentives to their employees?

1.2 Payment packages for salespeople are typically made up of salary and sales commission. The use of one or the other or both varies by industry. Look at the following figures. Can you suggest any reasons for the breakdown?

Industry	Salary	Commission	Combination
Aerospace	60%	—	40%
Appliances (household)	25%	25%	50%
Soft drinks	50%	—	50%
Cosmetics	33%	34%	33%
Food products	43%	14%	43%
Life insurance	20%	20%	60%
Radio and TV	—	—	100%
Tobacco	—	100%	—

How salespeople are paid by industry.
(In the aerospace industry, of the companies interviewed: 60% paid their salespeople by salary alone, none paid by commission alone, and 40% paid by a combination of salary and commission)

2 Reading

The following headings are guidelines for developing effective incentive plans. As you read, put them in their correct place in the text.

Study methods and procedures carefully
Set effective standards
The reward must be available to the employees
Guarantee an hourly base rate
Ensure that effort and rewards are directly related
The plan must be understandable and easily calculable by the employees
Guarantee your standards

DEVELOPING EFFECTIVE INCENTIVE PLANS

There are a number of reasons why incentive plans fail, most of which can be explained in terms of what we know about human motivation. For motivation to take place, the worker must believe that effort on his or her part will lead to reward, and he or she must want that reward. In most cases where incentive plans fails, it is because one or both of these conditions are not met. Unfair standards – standards that are too high or unattainable – are thus one cause for incentive plan failure. A second is the real or imagined fear that rates will be cut or standards raised if performance exceeds the standard for too long. Group restrictions and peer pressure can work both for and against the plan; if a group views the plan as fair, it can keep loafers in line and maintain high production. But the opposite is also true, and if for any reason the group views the plan as unfair it will – through education, ostracism or punishment – see that the production levels of group members are held down. Other plans fail because employees do not understand them, either because the plan is too complex or because it's not communicated to employees in an understandable way.

In summary, incentive plans can motivate employees. For example, two experts conclude that:

> There is considerable evidence that installation of such plans usually results in greater output per man-hour, lower unit costs, and higher wages in comparison with outcomes associated with the straight payment system.

But we also know that incentive plans can fail. So far we have discussed some of the causes of such failures. Now let us turn to some specific guidelines for developing effective incentive plans.

1. _____

The motivation model shows that for an incentive to motivate employees, they must see that effort will lead to their obtaining the reward. Your incentive plan should therefore reward employees in direct proportion to their increased productivity. Employees must also perceive they can actually do the tasks required. Thus, the standard has to be attainable, and you have to provide the necessary tools, equipment and training.

2. _____

For an incentive to motivate an employee, it is necessary to provide an attractive reward. Since people's needs differ, the attraction of various incentives also differs. Where other needs – for achievement, recognition, etc. – are paramount, financial incentives may have little or no effect on performance.

3. _____

Effective incentive plans are generally based on a meticulous work methods investigation. This usually requires the services of an industrial engineer or other methods expert. Through very careful observation and measurement they define fair performance standards. Your incentive plan is then built on these standards.

4. _____

Employees should be able to easily work out the rewards they will receive for various levels of effort (remember, it's very important for them to see the effort–reward link).

5. _____

The standards on which your incentive plan is built should satisfy the following requirements: they should be viewed as fair by your subordinates; they ought to be set high, but reasonable – there should be about a 50–50 chance of success at reaching them; and the goal should be specific – this is much more effective than telling someone to 'do your best'.

6. _____

Around the turn of the century employers often raised production standards whenever employees' pay became 'excessive'. Today, employees remain suspicious that exceeding the standard will result in raising the standards, and to protect their own long-term interests they don't produce above standard, and the incentive plan fails. Therefore, it's important that you view the standard as a contract with your employees. Once the plan is operational, you should use great caution before decreasing the size of the incentive in any way.

7. _____

Particularly for plant personnel, it's usually advisable to guarantee this rate for employees. They'll therefore know that no matter what happens they can at least earn a minimum guaranteed rate.

3 Comprehension/interpretation

3.1 What are the two requirements that must be satisfied for an employer to be motivated?
3.2 What will or is likely to happen if a group consider an incentive plan to be unfair?
3.3 How can one define fair performance standards?
3.4 Why is it dangerous to decrease the size of an incentive once it is operational?

4 Language focus

4.1 Advising and suggesting (see Unit 81 in *Language Reference for Business English*)

Look at the following sentences taken from the Reading passage:

'Your incentive plan *should* therefore reward employees in direct proportion to their increased productivity.'
'They *ought to* be set high, but reasonable – there *should* be about a 50–50 chance of success at reaching them . . .'

Now rewrite the following sentences using the word/construction shown in brackets. The first one has been done for you.

1. You should develop an effective incentive plan. (advise)
    I (would) advise you to develop an effective incentive plan.
2. I suggest you look at the area of human motivation. (recommend)
3. They advised us to set attainable standards. (suggest)
4. How about making the incentive plans simpler? (Why don't we)
5. Why don't you communicate the plan to the employees in an understandable way? (I think you should)

6. I think we should look at the reasons why incentive plans fail. (let's)
7. I think you should focus on some of the causes of failure. (How about)
8. I suggest that you prepare some specific guidelines for developing effective incentive plans. (advisable)
9. I suggest that you reward employees in direct proportion to their increased productivity. (ought to)
10. How about providing better tools, equipment and training? (Why don't you)
11. The methods expert advised him to provide an attractive reward. (suggest)
12. I suggest we build our incentive plans on fair performance standards. (let's)

4.2 Degree with **very** and **too** (see Unit 52 in *Language Reference for Business English*)

Look at the following sentences taken from the Reading passage:

'Other plans fail because employees do not understand them, either because the plan is *too* complex . . .'
'Through *very* careful observation and measurement they define fair performance standards.'
'Remember, it's *very* important for them to see the effort–reward link.'

Now complete the following sentences with either **very** or **too**:

1. These standards are _____ high for workers to achieve.
2. The standards are _____ unfair because they are unattainable.
3. _____ careful observation is required to define fair performance standards.
4. It should not be _____ difficult for the employees to work out the rewards they will receive.
5. It is _____ important for workers to see the link between effort and reward.
6. The goals should be _____ specific – so that each worker clearly knows what is expected.
7. Many workers fear that if performance standards become _____ high, then standards generally will be raised.
8. Although incentive plans present problems, managers are still _____ fascinated by them.
9. If one worker works _____ hard, there will be considerable pressure to reduce performance.
10. Incentive plans can be used for _____ many purposes, including reducing absenteeism.

5 Word study

The following exercise is based on opposites. The words on the left are taken from the text; the words on the right are their opposites. Match each word with its opposite.

1. fail		a.	false
2. raise		b.	trusting
3. high		c.	simple
4. exceed		d.	lower
5. true		e.	succeed
6. complex		f.	low
7. considerable		g.	maximum
8. reasonable		h.	fall below
9. suspicious		i.	unfair
10. minimum		j.	little

6 Transfer

The traditional approach at Codix has been to provide a guaranteed flat hourly rate and an overtime rate. There have been no incentive schemes for production workers. As employee relations manager, you are interested in discussing the introduction of an incentive scheme, but you think that it will be received with mistrust by the workers.

Discuss with your personal management team how best to present the benefits and operation of an incentive scheme.

Part 2: Reducing management fringe benefits

1 Warm-up

1.1 What is the difference between incentives and benefits?

1.2 In the UK we talk about executive perks, i.e. those fringe benefits added into the remuneration package to make it more attractive. In your country, is it normal practice to offer fringe benefits to executive and management personnel? If so, what are the typical perks offered?

2 Listening

After John Graham's presentation on the contract for payment, the questions and the discussion moves into the area of fringe benefits. You are a member of the audience. As you listen, complete Chart 6.3.

Chart 6.3   Fringe benefits

1. General points
   - They must be firmly incorporated within _____
   - They must be administered by the _____
2. Recommended action
   - _____
   - Personnel department to take control
3. General questions to justify their existence
   - _____
   - _____
   - _____
   - Is that purpose/benefit to the organisation worth achieving?
4. Administrative questions
   - _____
   - _____
5. _____
   - _____
   - _____

3 *Comprehension/interpretation*

3.1   Why is John pessimistic about personnel taking control of fringe benefits?

3.2   Why are many of the benefits offered?

3.3   Why is it difficult to ensure that the perk offered is for the benefit of the company?

3.4   What does John say can happen if fringe benefits are not managed positively?

4 Language focus

4.1 Questions and requests (see Units 38 and 82 in *Language Reference for Business English*)

Look at the following sentences taken from the Listening passage:

> '*Does it achieve its purpose?*'
> '*How much trouble does it cause?*'
> '*I'd like to ask you what you suggest that we do about them or with them.*'
> '*But could you tell me why it's offered?*'

Now rewrite the following direct questions as indirect (polite) questions. Use the notes given to make the polite formula. The first one has been done for you.

1. What do you think about the cost factor of fringe benefits? (you tell me)
   Can/Will/Could you tell me what you think about the cost factor of fringe benefits?
2. Would you suggest that companies get rid of fringe benefits? (like to know)
3. Why does a company provide a benefit such as membership of a health club? (would you mind)
4. Did the company provide the benefits just because it was accepted practice? (happen to know)
5. How are we going to take over control of fringe benefits? (please tell me)
6. Does each benefit achieve its purpose? (you tell me)
7. How does the organisation benefit from the fringe benefit? (happen to know)
8. How did they administer the fringe benefits? (would you mind)
9. How have our fringe benefits grown without any control at all? (like to ask)
10. How much does each feature cost? (tell us)

4.2 Question types (see Skill 2 in *Language Reference for Business English*)

Look at the following questions taken from the Listening passage:

> '*So does that answer your question?*' (closed)
> '*So, I'd like to ask you what you suggest that we do about them or with them?*' (encouraging)
> '*Why exactly do you say that?*' (probing)
> '*So, you'd advise us to take over control of the fringe benefit schemes in our companies.*' (leading)

Classify the following questions according to type:

1. Who should take over responsibility for fringe benefits?
2. I'd very much like to know who you think should administer fringe benefits.
3. How do you react to those who say that fringe benefits should be got rid of?
4. So, from your remarks you seem to be in favour of getting rid of fringe benefits.
5. Could you tell us why, exactly, you are so against fringe benefits?
6. Are fringe benefits a waste of money or a good investment?

Now imagine you are talking to someone about pension plans. Write six questions that you would ask, using each of the above question types.

5 *Word study*

The following two exercises are based on opposites. In the first exercise, form an opposite of the word given by adding a prefix. In the second exercise write the opposite of the word given.

5.1

1. agree
2. significant
3. incorporated
4. important
5. probably
6. appropriate
7. expensive
8. logically

5.2

1. pessimism
2. majority
3. general
4. health
5. forward
6. positively

6 *Transfer*

You are applying for a job as accounts manager at Codix and are at the point of negotiating your salary and benefits.

- Prepare the questions that you would ask your prospective employer concerning benefits.
- Describe the benefits package you would try to negotiate for yourself.

UNIT 7
Appraisal and career management

Section A: Appraisal

As the internal mail arrived from the personnel department the manager groaned, 'Surely it's not time to fill in all those appraisal forms again; they'll have to wait, I'm just too busy at the moment; waste of time anyway, nothing ever happens to them.' Appraisal done badly is a waste of time for everyone involved; appraisal done well can improve motivation and performance for both appraiser and appraisee, and can greatly assist both individual development and organisational planning.

Part 1: What is appraised?

1 Warm-up

1.1 What organisational decisions may be made on the basis of the performance appraisal?

1.2 How can the appraisal help the employee's performance?

2 Reading

As you read, complete Charts 7.1 and 7.2. In Chart 7.2, put ticks (✓) in the relevant columns.

WHAT IS APPRAISED?

Appraisal systems can measure a variety of things. They are sometimes designed to measure personality, sometimes behaviour or performance, and sometimes achievement of goals. These areas may be measured either quantitively or qualitatively. Qualitative appraisal often involves the writing of an unstructured narrative on the general performance of the appraisee. Alternatively, some guidance may be given as to the areas on which the appraiser should comment. The problems with qualitative appraisals are that they may leave important areas unappraised, and that they are not suitable for comparison purposes. When they are measured quantitively some form of scale is used, often comprising five categories of measurement from 'excellent', or 'always exceeds requirements' at one end to 'inadequate' or 'rarely meets requirements' at the other, with the mid-point being seen as acceptable. Scales are, however, not always constructed according to this plan. Sometimes on a five-point scale there will be four degrees of acceptable behaviour and only one that is unacceptable. Sometimes an even-numbered, usually a six-point, scale is used to prevent the tendency of raters to settle on the mid-point of the scale – either through lack of knowledge of the appraisee, lack of ability to discriminate, lack of confidence, or desire not to be too hard on appraisees. Rating other people is neither an easy nor a quick task, but it can be structured so that it is made as objective as possible.

Chart 7.1 Appraisal systems

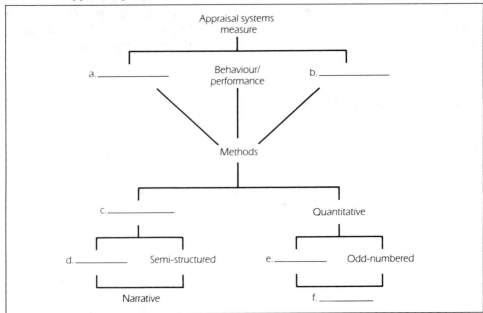

Much traditional appraisal was based on measures of personality traits that were felt to be important to the job. These included resourcefulness, enthusiasm, drive, application, and other traits such as intelligence. One difficulty with these is that everyone defines them differently, and the traits that are used are not always mutually exclusive. Raters, therefore, are often unsure of what they are rating. One helpful approach is to concentrate on the job rather than the person. In an attempt to do this, some organisations call their annual appraisal activity the 'job appraisal review'. Both the requirements of the job and the way that it is performed are considered.

Behaviourally anchored rating scales

This is one way of linking ratings to behaviour at work. At the first stage a sample group of raters suggest independently examples of behaviour for each point on a scale associated with a behavioural feature to be assessed, e.g. relations with clients. From this a wide variety of behavioural examples are collected. At the next stage these examples are collated, and then returned to the raters without any indication of the scale point for which they were suggested. The raters allocate a numerical scale point to each example, and those examples which are consistently located at the same point on the scale are selected to be used as the behavioural examples for that point on the scale. Future raters then have some guidance as to the type of behaviour that would be expected at each point. BARS are most helpful when using scales that relate more clearly to work behaviour rather than specific job performance.

A behaviourally anchored rating scale: relations with clients

Behavioural example	Points of the rating scale
Often makes telephone calls on behalf of the client to find the correct office for him to go to even though this is not part of the job.	1
Will often spend an hour with a client in order to get to the root of a very complex problem.	2
Usually remains calm when dealing with an irate client.	3
If the answer to the client's problem is not immediately to hand he often tells them he has not got the information.	4
Sometimes ignores clients waiting at the reception desk for up to ten minutes even when he is not busy with other work.	5
Regularly keeps clients waiting for ten minutes or more and responds to their questions with comments such as 'I can't be expected to know that' and 'You're not in the right place for that'.	6

Behavioural observation scales (BOS)

These are an alternative to BARS. They indicate a number of dimensions of performance with behavioural statements for each. Individuals are appraised as to the extent
to which they display each of the characteristics. An example of a behavioural
observation scale is shown below.

A behavioural observation scale

Leadership/staff supervision

1 Provides help, training and guidance so that employees can improve their
   performance.

   Almost never   5   4   3   2   1   Almost always

2 Explains to staff exactly what is expected of them – staff know their job
   responsibilities.

   Almost never   5   4   3   2   1   Almost always

3 Gets involved in subordinates' work only to check it.

   Almost never   5   4   3   2   1   Almost always

4 Consults staff for their ideas on ways of making their jobs better.

   Almost never   5   4   3   2   1   Almost always

5 Praises staff for things they do well.

   Almost never   5   4   3   2   1   Almost always

6 Passes important information to subordinates.

   Almost never   5   4   3   2   1   Almost always

The number of behavioural statements to be rated for any one dimension will be
determined through the job analysis used to identify the key dimensions of performance
and behavioural statements.

Meeting objectives (MO)

Another method of making appraisal more objective is to use the process to set job
objectives over the coming year and, a year later, to measure the extent to which these
objectives have been met. The extent to which the appraisee is involved in setting
these objectives varies considerably. If these objectives are part of an organisational
management by objectives (MBO) scheme, then the individual will never be involved
and will simply have them handed down. Alternatively, if they are not part of a larger
scheme, there is a lot of scope for the individual to participate in the setting of such
objectives. One of the biggest problems with appraisal on the basis of meeting
objectives is that factors beyond the employee's control may make the objectives more

difficult than anticipated, or even impossible. Another problem is that objectives will change over a period and so the original list is not so relevant a year later.

Development of appraisal criteria
Various methods have been suggested to identify appraisal criteria. These include the use of critical incident techniques to identify particularly difficult problems at work, content analysis of working documents, and performance questionnaires whereby managers and potential appraisees identify (anonymously) what characterises the most effective job-holder and the least effective job-holder.

Job analysis
In addition to identifying appraisal criteria, job analysis is used to formulate key tasks and duties, and the performance standards that are expected. Appraisal is then based on a comparison between this and the performance actually achieved. This is similar to appraisal by objectives, but much broader. This type of job analysis and appraisal is a very useful approach in smaller organisations which cannot afford to invest in the development of sophisticated appraisal criteria. It is an approach which has apparent validity and clearly relates to job performance.

Chart 7.2 Summary of appraisal methods

	Measure			Method	
	Personality	Behaviour	Achievement	Qualitative	Quantitative
BARS					
BOS					
MO					

3 Comprehension/interpretation

3.1 What two problems are associated with qualitative appraisals?
3.2 What two difficulties are associated with the criteria often found in personality appraisals?
3.3 What is one of the biggest problems with appraisal on the basis of meeting objectives?
3.4 What approach or document can be used to help identify performance appraisal criteria?

4 Language focus

4.1 Expressions of frequency (see Unit 51 in *Language Reference for Business English*)

Look at the following sentences taken from the Reading passage:

'The traits that are used are not *always* mutually exclusive.'
'Qualitative appraisal *often* involves the writing of an unstructured narrative on the general performance of the appraisee.'
'They are *sometimes* designed to measure personality, *sometimes* behaviour or performance, and *sometimes* achievement of goals.'

Complete the following sentences using an appropriate word or phrase of indefinite frequency with the meaning given. Your words may be adjectives or adverbs. The first one has been done for you.

1. In appraisals managers *occasionally* fail to differentiate between current performance and potential performance. (50%)
2. As a result managers are _ _ _ _ _ _ _ _ _ _ promoted to positions in which they cannot perform adequately. (40%)
3. The _ _ _ _ _ _ _ _ _ approach is the superior's rating of subordinates. (90%)
4. A group of superiors rating subordinates is also _ _ _ _ _ _ _ _ _ _ used for appraisal. (75%)
5. A group of peers rating a colleague is _ _ _ _ _ _ _ _ _ _ used in business organisations. (25%)
6. A fourth approach – subordinates' rating of bosses – is _ _ _ _ _ _ _ _ _ _ used. (10%)
7. _ _ _ _ _ _ _ _ _ _ _, appraisals concentrate on personal characteristics such as intelligence, decisiveness, creativity, and ability to get along with others. (90%)
8. There are _ _ _ _ _ _ _ _ _ _ pitfalls in carrying out appraisals. (100%)
9. Managers should _ _ _ _ _ _ _ _ _ _ allow their personal biases to interfere with rating. (0%)
10. The employee should _ _ _ _ _ _ _ _ _ _ be an equal and active partner with the manager throughout the appraisal process. (100%)

4.2 **Both, either** and **neither** (see Unit 60 in *Language Reference for Business English*)

Look at the following sentences taken from the Reading passage:

> '*Both* the requirements of the job and the way that it is performed are considered.'
> 'These areas may be measured *either* quantitively *or* qualitatively.'
> 'Rating other people is *neither* an easy *nor* a quick task.'

Now complete the following sentences by adding the appropriate words based on both grammatical accuracy and your knowledge of the subject:

1. Performance appraisal is one of the most difficult tasks a manager has to carry out; _____ the appraisal itself _____ the communication of the results are easy.
2. Appraisal is the continuous process of feeding back information to subordinates about how well they are doing; it happens _____ informally _____ systematically.
3. In the case of informal appraisal the manager spontaneously mentions that a piece of work has been done _____ well _____ poorly.
4. Because of the close connection between the behaviour and the feedback on it, informal appraisal _____ encourages desirable performance _____ discourages undesirable performance before it becomes engrained.
5. A company's employees must see appraisal _____ as an important activity _____ as an integral part of the organisation's culture.
6. In most major organisations formal appraisals are carried out _____ once _____ twice a year.
7. To be effective, the appraisal method must be perceived by subordinates as based on _____ uniform _____ fair standards.
8. Managers should not allow _____ race, colour, sex _____ religion to influence their judgement.
9. _____ age, style of clothing _____ political viewpoint should be allowed to interfere.
10. The halo effect is a common tendency to rate subordinates _____ high _____ low on all performance measures based on one of their characteristics.

5 Word study

The following exercise is based on grouping words into categories based on shared associations. There are three categories:

- Words describing personal qualities (P)
- Words associated with quantitive assessment (Q)
- Words connected with handling the data (D)

Write the appropriate letter next to each of the following words:

1. drive
2. scale
3. select
4. assess
5. personality
6. degree
7. measure
8. measurement
9. intelligence
10. resourcefulness
11. collate
12. analyse
13. rating
14. allocate
15. point
16. enthusiasm
17. identify
18. application

6 Transfer

Use the following BOS to evaluate your trainer. First complete the table individually; then discuss your evaluation in small groups. Finally, you may wish to give some feedback to your trainer.

INSTRUCTOR

DEPARTMENT

COURSE NUMBER OR TITLE

I The following items reflect some of the ways teachers can be described in and out of the classroom. For the instructor named above, please circle the number that indicates the degree to which you feel each item is descriptive of him or her. In some cases, the statement may not apply to this individual. In these cases, tick *Doesn't apply or don't know* for that item.

		Doesn't apply or don't know
1.	Has command of the subject, presents material in an analytic way, contrasts various points of view, discusses current developments, and relates topics to other areas of knowledge.	Almost never 5 4 3 2 1 Almost always	( )
2.	Makes himself clear, states objectives, summarises major points, presents material in an organised manner, and provides emphasis.	Almost never 5 4 3 2 1 Almost always	( )
3.	Is sensitive to the response of the class, encourages student participation, and welcomes questions and discussion.	Almost never 5 4 3 2 1 Almost always	( )
4.	Is available to and friendly towards students, is interested in students as individuals, is himself respected as a person, and is valued for advice not directly related to the course.	Almost never 5 4 3 2 1 Almost always	( )
5.	Enjoys teaching, is enthusiastic about his subject, makes the course exciting, and has self-confidence.	Almost never 5 4 3 2 1 Almost always	( )

Note: Additional items may be presented by instructor and/or department.

Adapted from *Developing Programs for Faculty Evaluation*, Richard Miller (San Francisco: Jossey-Bass, 1974), p. 43.

Part 2: Setting up an appraisal system

1 Warm-up

1.1 What are the purposes of the appraisal interview?
1.2 How should the appraisee ideally feel at the end of the interview?

2 Listening

The following extract is taken from a workshop on appraisal criteria that Philip Bradshaw is running for junior managers. As you listen, write down in Chart 7.3 the criteria that Philip puts on the flipchart. Then add for each point whether, in your opinion, it is something that is important for appraiser, appraisee or organisation.

Chart 7.3 Appraisal criteria

Conditions	Important to:		
	Appraiser	Appraisee	Organisation
1. ————————			
2. ————————			
3. ————————			
4. ————————			
————————			
5. ————————			
6. ————————			
————————			
7. ————————			

3 Comprehension/interpretation

3.1 In the discussion on ease of administration, what two problem areas for the appraiser are mentioned?
3.2 What should the appraisee feel to be fair and justified?
3.3 What two examples are given of failure due to circumstances beyond the appraisee's control?
3.4 What factor may cause a change in the action plan?

4 Language focus

4.1 The language of meetings (see Skill 2 in *Language Reference for Business English*)

Look at the following sentences taken from the Listening passage:

> '*Shall we get started?*'
> '*Anyway, in today's session I'd like to consider how to set up a useful and workable appraisal system.*'
> '*Simon, would you like to start?*'
> '*Yes, can you say a bit more about that?*'

In the list on the left are some phrases and sentences from the meeting. On the right are the purposes of these phrases and sentences. Link each phrase/sentence with its purpose. Each purpose may be used more than one. The first one has been done for you.

1. Let's start by looking at . . .	a. Asking for acknowledgement
2. Anything else?	b. Starting on the first point
3. What do the others think?	c. Summarising
4. Does that cover your point?	d. Not understanding
5. Okay, I think that covers . . .	e. Bringing people in
6. Shall we get started?	f. Acknowledging information
7. Yes, that's fine/right.	g. Moving on
8. In today's session I'd like to consider . . .	h. Ending (one part of) the session
9. Yes, go on. (informal)	i. Asking for examples
10. Can you say a bit more about that?	j. Asking for more information
11. Sorry, I'm not with you.	k. Asking for contributions
12. For instance?	l. Opening the meeting
13. Simon, would you like to start?	
14. Can we move on to another point?	
15. Yes/Right/Fine/Okay	
16. Now let's have a look at what we've got so far.	

1. *b*

4.2 Verbs of speaking (see Unit 24 in *Language Reference for Business English*)

Look at the following extracts taken from the Listening passage:

> 'In the last session we *talked* about what is appraised . . .'
> 'We *said* that one of the points was ease of administration.'
> 'If we *tell* one of our production workers to do something . . .'
> 'So, I'd like you now to . . . spend five minutes *discussing* the conditions that must be met.'

Now complete the following sentences, writing in an appropriate verb or preposition, where necessary:

1. He _____ us that some managers rate each subordinate by different standards.
2. He _____ to us _____ shifting standards.
3. He _____ that to be effective, the appraisal method must be seen to be fair.
4. Then we discussed _____ the problem of personal bias.
5. He _____ to us _____ how personal biases distort ratings.
6. He _____ that an increasing number of organisations deal with the problem of bias by asking for explanations of ratings.
7. Then we _____ about rating styles.
8. He talked _____ the different patterns of raters; some rate harshly, others rate easily.
9. He _____ us that the lack of uniform rating standards is unfair to employees.
10. We _____ to him that we thought it was also unfair to organisations.
11. We _____ how top management should integrate performance appraisal into the overall culture.
12. Finally we _____ how to make the employee an equal and active partner with the manager throughout the process.

5 Word study

Complete the word table below.

Noun	Adjective	Adverb
_____	useful	usefully
_____	easy	_____
efficiency	_____	_____
_____	_____	separately
_____	_____	fairly
_____	relevant	_____
_____	_____	presumably
_____	broad	_____
success	_____	_____
_____	responsible	_____

6 Transfer

Imagine that you participated in the workshop that you listened to in this session. At the end of the workshop Philip Bradshaw asked you to draft a short report of the proceedings as a record of what was discussed and for circulation amongst the participants.

Section B: Career planning and management

Activities like screening, training and appraising serve two basic functions in an organisation. First, their traditional function has been to staff the organisation – to fill its open positions with employees who have the requisite interests, abilities and skills. Increasingly, however, these activities are taking on a second role – that of ensuring that the long-term interests of the employees are protected by the organisation and that, in particular, the employee is encouraged to grow and realise his or her full potential. Referring to personnel management as human resource planning and development reflects this second role. The basic, if implicit, assumption underlying the focus on human resource planning and development is, thus, that the organisation has an obligation to utilise its employees' abilities to the fullest and to give every employee an opportunity to grow and to realise his or her full potential.

Part 1: The stages in a person's career

1 Warm-up

1.1   What are the benefits to the employee of the increased emphasis on career planning and development?

1.2   What are the possible benefits to the employer of the increased emphasis on career planning and development?

2 Reading

Each person's career goes through stages, and it is important to understand how careers evolve. One reason is that you can better plan your own career and deal with occasional career crises if and when they occur. Another is because it can improve your own performance by giving you a better insight into your employees' behaviour. The main stages of one's career can be summarised as follows.

As you read, label each stage and substage with its appropriate title from the following list:

Stages	Substages
Maintenance	Stabilisation
Decline	Mid-career crisis
Exploration	Trial
Establishment	
Growth	

_____ stage

During this stage (from birth to age 14) the person develops a self-concept by identifying with and interacting with other people such as family, friends and teachers. Towards the beginning of this period, role-playing is important, and children experiment with different ways of acting; this helps them to form impressions of how other people react to different behaviours, and contributes to their developing a unique self-concept, or identity. Towards the end of this stage, the adolescent (who by this time has developed some preliminary ideas of what his or her interests and abilities are) begins some realistic thinking about alternative occupations.

_____ stage

During this stage (from 15 to 24) the person seriously explores various occupational alternatives, attempting to match these alternatives with what he or she has learned about them (and about his or her own interests and abilities from school, leisure activities, and part-time work). Some tentative broad occupational choices are usually made during the beginning of this period. This choice is, then refined as the person learns more about the choice and about himself, until, before the end of this period, a seemingly appropriate choice is made and the person tries for a first job.

Probably the most important task the person has in this and the preceding stage is that of developing a realistic understanding of his or her abilities and talents. Similarly, the person must discover and develop his or her values, motives and ambitions, and make sound educational decisions based on reliable sources of information about occupational alternatives.

_____ stage

This stage (from about 24 to 44) is the heart of most people's working lives. Sometimes during this period (and, it is to be hoped, towards the beginning) a suitable occupation is found and the person engages in those activities that help him or her to earn a permanent place in it. Often (and particularly in the professions) the person locks on to a chosen occupation early. But in most cases, this is the period during which the person is continually testing his or her capabilities and ambitions against those of the initial occupational choice. This stage itself comprises three substages.

_____ substage

This lasts from about 25 to 30; during this period the person determines whether or not the chosen field is suitable; if it is not, several changes might be attempted.

_____ substage

This lasts from about 30 to 40. During this period firm occupational goals are set, while at the same time the person does more explicit career planning to determine the sequence of promotions, job changes and/or any educational activities that seem necessary for accomplishing these goals.

_____ substage

Finally, somewhere between the mid-thirties and mid-forties people often made a major reassessment of their progress relative to original ambitions and goals. They may find that they are not going to realise their dreams or that, having accomplished what they set out to do, their dreams are not all they were made out to be. Also, during this period, people have to decide how important work and career are to be in their total life. It is often during this substage that a person is, for the first time, faced with the difficult decisions of what he or she really wants, what really can be accomplished, and how much must be sacrificed to achieve this.

_____ stage

Between the ages of 45 and 65, many people slide into this stage. During this period the person has typically created for himself or herself a place in the world of work and most efforts are now directed to securing that place.

_____ stage

As retirement approaches, there is often a deceleration period during which many people are faced with the prospect of having to accept reduced levels of power and responsibility, and have to learn to accept and develop new roles as mentor and confidant for those who are younger. There is, then, the more-or-less inevitable retirement. After this, the person is faced with the prospect of finding alternative uses for the time and effort formerly expended on his or her occupation.

3 Comprehension/interpretation

3.1 When does a person begin to develop ideas about possible jobs?
3.2 What is the most important task in the first two stages?
3.3 When do professional people usually engage upon their chosen occupation?
3.4 Why is the decline stage associated with deceleration?

4 Language focus

4.1 Prepositions of time (see Unit 63 in *Language Reference for Business English*)

Look at the following sentences taken from the Reading passage:

'*After* this, the person is faced with the prospect of finding alternative uses for the time and effort formerly expended on his or her occupation.'
'*Before* the end of this period, a seemingly appropriate choice is made and the person tries for a first job.'
'*During* this period the person has typically created for himself or herself a place in the world of work . . .'

Now complete the following sentences with an appropriate preposition of time:

It is now rare for people to retire abruptly 1. _____ working at high pressure 2. _____ the very end. 3. _____ the months 4. _____ retirement, some sort of phased withdrawal is organised so that the retiree is prepared to bow out 5. _____ his or her retirement day. And advantage of this arrangement is that there may be 'a life 6. _____ death', 7. _____ which the retiree continues to work part-time. Examples are that the retiree may come back to help out 8. _____ peak periods or 9. _____ holiday times. Many organisations go to great lengths to keep in touch with their retired personnel, arranging parties 10. _____ Christmas, excursions 11. _____ summer and other activities 12. _____ the evenings or 13. _____ weekends.

It is not, of course, possible to draw state retirement pension in the UK 14. _____ the official retirement ages of 60 or 65; however, 15. _____ the time retirement approaches many people who have worked 16. _____ most of their lives will accept an occupational pension and a lump sum. Thus, 17. _____ their sixties, many can look forward to a new lease of life and the opportunity to pursue other interests or start their own business.

4.2 Clauses of time (see Unit 43 in *Language Reference for Business English*)

Look at the following sentences taken from the Listening passage:

> '*As retirement approaches*, there is often a deceleration period . . .'
> 'One reason is that you can better plan your own career and deal with occasional career crises if and *when they occur.*'
> 'During this period firm occupational goals are set, *while at the same time the person does more explicit career planning* . . .'

Now complete the following sentences with an appropriate conjunction of time:

1. _ _ _ _ _ _ _ _ _ _ going to an interview, make sure you have done all the necessary preparation.
2. Don't go to an interview _ _ _ _ _ _ _ _ _ _ you have done all the necessary preparation.
3. _ _ _ _ _ _ _ _ _ _ answering the first questions, be as brief as possible.
4. Get your interviewer to describe the company's needs _ _ _ _ _ _ _ _ _ _ you can.
5. _ _ _ _ _ _ _ _ _ _ having found out the company's needs, relate yourself to those needs.
6. Now describe your own achievements _ _ _ _ _ _ _ _ _ _ keeping in mind those needs.
7. _ _ _ _ _ _ _ _ _ _ answering, pause to make sure you understand what the interviewer wants.
8. _ _ _ _ _ _ _ _ _ _ answering, try to emphasise how you will help the interviewer solve his or her problem.

9. _ _ _ _ _ _ _ _ _ _ you go for an interview, remember the importance of appearance.
10. In 80 per cent of cases interviewers make up their minds in the first few minutes _ _ _ _ _ _ _ _ _ the interview starts.
11. A good first impression may turn to bad _ _ _ _ _ _ _ _ _ _ the interview is in progress.
12. But remember that _ _ _ _ _ _ _ _ _ _ formed, bad impressions are almost impossible to overcome.

5 Word study

Although most nouns form the plural by adding an **s** to the singular, e.g. *manager* → *managers*, there are some notable exceptions, e.g. *crisis* → *crises*. What are the plurals of the following?

life   _____
stimulus   _____
bonus   _____
curriculum   _____
index   _____
information   _____
basis   _____
criterion   _____
analysis   _____
appendix   _____
formula   _____
diploma   _____
belief   _____
advice   _____
medium   _____

6 Transfer

If you could have any kind of job, what would it be? Invent your own job if need be, and don't worry about what you can do – just what you want to do.

Part 2: Identifying your occupational orientation

1 Warm-up

1.1 Successful job performance doesn't only depend on motivation. What other factors are involved?

1.2 To what extent were these a factor in your job/study choice?

2 Listening

The following extract is taken from a workshop on identifying occupational orientations that Philip Bradshaw is running for junior managers. As you listen, write down in Chart 7.4 the personality orientations and the jobs associated with them.

Chart 7.4   Personality orientations and associated jobs

Personality orientations	Associated jobs
1. _____	_____
2. _____	_____
3. _____	_____
4. _____	_____
5. _____	_____
6. _____	_____

3 Comprehension/interpretation

3.1 What abilities do conventional people have?

3.2 What are the two 'people' orientations.

3.3 What 'people' skill do enterprising people have?

3.4 What abilities do realistic people have?

4 Language focus

4.1 Likes and preferences (see Units 12, 14 and 74 in *Language Reference for Business English*)

Look at the following sentences taken from the Listening passage:

'I *like* to work with people.'
'Firstly, I *like* working with data . . .'
'They . . . *enjoy* carrying things out in detail or following through other people's instructions.
'I *don't mind* participating in training courses, but I'm not much good at training people myself.'

Now complete the following sentences with an appropriate form of the verbs given in brackets:

1. In today's session I _ _ _ _ _ _ _ _ _ _ at career planning. (like)
2. People naturally _ _ _ _ _ _ _ _ _ _ in jobs that they are interested in and which they have the skills for. (enjoy/excel)
3. First of all, you should divide into your groups and spend a little discussing your own personal orientation or orientations – in other words what you _ _ _ _ _ _ _ _ _ _. (like/do)
4. Generally at that stage I _ _ _ _ _ _ _ _ _ _ some feedback from the groups. (like/get)
5. A: Okay, Sheila, _ _ _ _ _ _ _ _ _ _ you _ _ _ _ _ _ _ _ _ _? (like/start)
   B: Well, actually, I _ _ _ _ _ _ _ _ _ _. (prefer not)
6. A: Well, if you _ _ _ _ _ _ _ _ _ _ (enjoy/work) with people, I think you _ _ _ _ _ _ _ _ _ _ (enjoy/work) in personnel.
7. In general I _ _ _ _ _ _ _ _ _ _ (not mind/sit) in front of a computer; on the other hand I _ _ _ _ _ _ _ _ _ _ (not/really/like/train) people myself.
8. Well, we recognise two types of personality: 'conventional' people who _ _ _ _ _ _ _ _ _ _ (like/work) with data; they _ _ _ _ _ _ _ _ _ _ (like/other people/give) them instructions.
9. On the other hand we have 'investigative' people, who _ _ _ _ _ _ _ _ _ _ others. (prefer/observe)
10. I _ _ _ _ _ _ _ _ _ _ (not mind/other people/help) me, but I _ _ _ _ _ _ _ _ _ _ (prefer/solve) problems on my own.

4.2   Suggesting (see Unit 81 in *Language Reference for Business English*)

Look at the following sentences taken from the Listening passage:

'*Shall* we get started?'
'So *let's* say fifteen minutes to discuss that . . .'
'*How about* banking?'

Now rewrite the following sentences using the words/construction given in brackets. The first one has been done for you.

1. Shall we get started? (I suggest)
   I suggest that we (should) get started.
2. I suggest that we kick off with a brainstorming session. (how about)
3. I recommend that we look at how to plan a career first. (let's)
4. I would advise you to learn as much as you can about their interests, aptitudes and skills. (suggest)
5. I would recommend that you begin your career planning by learning about yourselves. (advise)
6. So, first I think you should discuss your own personal orientation or orientations. (why don't you)
7. So let's spend fifteen minutes on that. (ought)

8. He suggested that I should not train others. (advise)
9. Why don't you try banking? (how about)
10. Now, I suggest that we look at these in more detail. (let's)

5 Word study

In the verb phrases below the particle after the verb (either a preposition or adverb is missing). Complete the phrases by selecting one of the particles from the following list. You should use each particle only one.

about   at   in   into   out
through   with   with   up

1. to work _____ machines
2. to divide _____ groups
3. to learn _____ their interests
4. to look _____ the area of appraisal
5. to deal _____ people
6. to set _____ an appraisal system
7. to follow _____ instructions
8. to seek _____ jobs
9. to be interested _____ jobs
10. to come up _____ different features.

6 Transfer

One useful exercise for identifying occupational skills is to write a short essay describing the most enjoyable occupational tasks you have had. (Notice it is *tasks*, not *job*.) Go into as much detail as you can about your duties and responsibilities, and especially what you found enjoyable in each task. Then do the same thing for two other tasks. Finally, go through your three essays and underline the skills that you mentioned most often.

UNIT 8
The legal environment

Section A: Labour relations

Trade union recognition is widespread in Britain, although there has been a drop of over two million members since 1980. Furthermore, much of the expansion in the economy is in companies that are electing not to recognise trade unions. Some personnel managers are in establishments where unions are not recognised and where recognition is unlikely, some are in establishments where they are working towards recognition, but the great majority are in a situation where unions are recognised to some degree for at least part of the workforce. Thus most personnel managers are in a situation where they have to continue to manage recognition rather than initiate or reject it.

Part 1: Trade union recognition

1 *Warm-up*

1.1   Is union membership increasing or decreasing in your country?
1.2   What are the reasons for this situation?

2 Reading

As you read, complete Chart 8.1 at the end of the text.

When a trade union has recruited a number of members in an organisation it will seek recognition from the employer in order to represent those members. The step of recognition is seldom easy but is very important as it marks an irrevocable movement away from unilateral decision-making by the management. We can examine some of the questions to be considered.

WHY SHOULD A UNION BE RECOGNISED AT ALL?

If the employees want that type of representation they will not readily co-operate with the employer if he refuses. In extreme cases this can generate sufficient antagonism to cause industrial action in support of recognition. A more positive reason is the benefits that can flow from recognition: there are employee representatives with whom to discuss, consult and negotiate so that communication and working relationships can be improved. Recent years have, however, certainly seen a decline in union membership and effectiveness in resisting management initiatives. Employers are considering union recognition claims more carefully and collective consent (the acceptance of a general framework of rules and guidelines within which management and employees operate) can be achieved by other means in some situations, providing that the management work hard at the job of securing and maintaining that consent.

WHEN SHOULD A UNION BE RECOGNISED?

When it has sufficient support from the employees. There is no simple way of determining what is sufficient. The 1971 Industrial Relations Act specified that 51 per cent of the employees must be in membership, but current legislation lays down no percentage. The first thirteen cases brought to ACAS (Advisory, Conciliation and Arbitration Service) after the passing of the Employment Protection Act 1975 produced recommendations for recognition where the level of membership varied from 21 per cent to 100 per cent, and in five cases the figure was below 40 per cent. Among the factors that influenced ACAS whether or not to recommend recognition was the degree of union organisation and efficiency, the size of the constituency and the degree of opposition from non-union employees. A common reason for the management of an organisation to recognise a union relatively quickly is where there is the possibility of competing claims, with some employees seeking to get another union established because they do not like the first.

FOR WHOM SHOULD A UNION BE RECOGNISED?

For that group of employees who have a sufficient commonality of interests, terms and conditions for one union to be able to represent them and the management be able to respond. This group of employees is sometimes described as those making up a bargaining unit; the boundaries of the units need careful consideration by the management to determine what is most appropriate and what consequent response to recognition claims they will make. There are a number of boundaries that are generally acknowledged: manual employees are usually represented by different unions from white-collar employees, and skilled employees are sometimes represented by a different union from the semi-skilled and unskilled as well as from those possessing different skills. Other boundaries are less easy, particularly where a distinction may be drawn on the grounds of hierarchical status, as between those who are paid monthly and those paid weekly. Where status is related to responsibility for subordinates, there appears to be another accepted boundary: the supervisor will not be represented by the same union as the supervised, although one or two levels may be included sometimes in the same unit.

FOR WHAT SHOULD A UNION BE RECOGNISED?
The terms and conditions of employment of the employees who are members of the bargaining unit. A union can seek recognition on anything that might be covered in a contract of employment, but the employer may agree to recognition only for a limited range of topics. The irreducible minimum is assistance by a union representative for members with grievances, but the extent to which matters beyond that are recognised as being a subject of bargaining depends on which consent category the organisation is in. It also depends on the possible existence of other agreements that could take some matters out of the scope of local recognition.

Chart 8.1   Summary table on union recognition

Why?	1.	To gain _____ employer
	2.	To gain _____ , e.g. employee representatives with whom to _____
When?	1.	Union has _____
	2.	Sufficient support depends on:
		a. _____
		b. _____
		c. _____ from non-union employees
For whom?	1.	That group of employees who have _____ _____
	2.	This group is called a _____
For what?	1.	_____ of the employees who are members of the bargaining unit
	2.	Possible range is anything in _____ , but minimum is assistance by a union representative for _____ _____

3 Comprehension/interpretation

3.1 In what way does union recognition mark an irrevocable step for management?

3.2 In the 1980s in Britain, in what ways have employers responded to claims for union recognition?

3.3 What may influence management to recognise one union quickly?

3.4 List three factors that may determine the boundaries between bargaining units?

4 Language focus

4.1 Review of modals (see Units 16–20 in *Language Reference for Business English*)

Look at the following sentences taken from the Reading passage:

'A more positive reason is the benefits that *can* flow from recognition.'
'Fifty-one per cent of the employees *must* be in membership.'
'The employer *may* agree to recognition only for a limited range of topics.'
'Why *should* a union be recognised at all?'

Now complete the following sentences with an appropriate modal which expresses the meaning shown in brackets. The first one has been done for you.

1. If your trade union *can* (ability) recruit enough members, it *should* (advice) seek recognition from the employer in order to represent those members.
2. The step of recognition _____ (strong possibility) be difficult.
3. There are cases where the employer _____ (no willingness) agree to union recognition; in this situation the workers often _____ (no willingness) co-operate with management.
4. In extreme cases this _____ (weak possibility) lead to industrial action in support of recognition.
5. Recognition _____ (no necessity) be seen as bringing drawbacks to an organisation.
6. In fact employee representatives _____ (possibility) often improve communication and working relationships.
7. Unions today _____ (necessity) fight against the decline in union membership.
8. Employers _____ (no necessity) accept union recognition as the only way of securing the support of the workforce.
9. A union _____ (weak possibility) be recognised with less than 40 per cent support.
10. A union _____ (impossibility) be recognised without a degree of union organisation and efficiency.
11. A union _____ (prohibition) seek recognition on matters outside a contract of employment.
12. Other agreements _____ (weak possibility) take some matters out of the scope of union recognition.

4.2   Tense review (see Unit 11 in *Language Reference for Business English*)

Look at the following sentences taken from the Reading passage:

> 'Employers *are considering* union recognition claims more carefully . . .'
> 'Where status is related to responsibility for subordinates, there *appears* to be another accepted boundary . . .'
> 'The 1971 Industrial Relations Act *specified* that 51 per cent of the employees must be in membership . . .'
> 'Recent years *have*, however, certainly *seen* a decline in union membership.'

Now complete the following sentences by putting the verbs in brackets into the correct tense:

1. At present we _ _ _ _ _ _ _ _ _ _ (recruit) as many members as possible in order to seek union recognition.
2. Last year we _ _ _ _ _ _ _ _ _ _ (announce) to management our decision to seek union recognition.
3. Up to now management _ _ _ _ _ _ _ _ _ _ (react) very well to our requests.
4. If the situation _ _ _ _ _ _ _ _ _ _ (not change), we expect to get recognition within the next few months.
5. I think that over the last few months management_ _ _ _ _ _ _ _ _ _(recognise) the benefits that arise as a result of union recognition.
6. Management announced that, although earlier they _ _ _ _ _ _ _ _ _ _ (view) union recognition as a threat, they now _ _ _ _ _ _ _ _ _ _ (see) it as a positive step.
7. In fact their positive attitude became clear while we _ _ _ _ _ _ _ _ _ _ (discuss) the steps to be taken.
8. We expect that white collar workers and manual workers _ _ _ _ _ _ _ _ _ _ (represent) by different unions.
9. However, we don't propose to distinguish between skilled and semi-skilled workers; if the two categories _ _ _ _ _ _ _ _ _ _ (separate), we think it _ _ _ _ _ _ _ _ _ _ (make) the situation too complicated.
10. We _ _ _ _ _ _ _ _ _ _ (still think) about what areas should form the basis for recognition.

5 Word study

Nouns can be divided into concrete nouns and abstract nouns. Within the first category we recognise things, animals and people; within the second we include nouns which refer to states, events and feelings. Thus, if we take the verb recruit, there are two nouns associated with it – recruiter (concrete) and recruitment (abstract). Write down the abstract nouns from the following verbs:

Verbs	Nouns
represent	_____
recognise	_____
refuse	_____
discuss	_____
consult	_____
initiate	_____
achieve	_____
maintain	_____
vary	_____
encourage	_____
consider	_____
distinguish	_____
employ	_____
antagonise	_____

6 Transfer

We can generalise by saying that unions have two sets of aims: one for union security, and the other for improved wages, hours, working conditions and benefits for their members. Discuss to what extent the employees in your organisation are fighting for or looking for changes in any of the above areas.

Part 2: Conflict – sources, benefits and drawbacks

1 Warm-up

1.1 After union recognition the key aspects of the employer–employee relationship can no longer be decided unilaterally. What are these key aspects?

1.2 How must these matters be settled after union recognition?

2 Listening

As in most organisations, the line managers in Codix are necessarily responsible for industrial relations in their particular areas of operations. They need the freedom to manage their departments or sections effectively according to agreed policies and with access to specialist advice. In this case the specialist advice comes from John Wheeler, the employee relations manager. In this extract you will hear the introduction to John's talk to line managers about conflict within the organisation.

As you listen, complete Chart 8.2 summarising John's main points.

Chart 8.2 Conflict

```
1.  Causes

    a.  _____

    b.  A divergence of interests between managers and non-managers

    c.  _____ between managers and non-managers

    d.  _____

    e.  Tradition

2.  Benefits

    a.  Can _____

    b.  Can lead to the introduction of new rules

    c.  Can _____

    d.  Can lead the parties to understand their respective positions

3.  Drawbacks

    a.  _____

    b.  _____ for the participants

    c.  Organisational _____

    d.  Risk of _____

    e.  Worsening communication
```

3 Comprehension/interpretation

3.1 What three activities does John mention that provide vicarious outlets for our aggressive drive?

3.2 One source of conflict is the urge to compete. For what?

3.3 Which formal rule does John mention as an example?

3.4 What five examples of organisational stress and inefficiency does John mention?

4 Language focus

4.1 Comparing and contrasting ideas (see Unit 72 in *Language Reference for Business English*)

Look at the following sentences taken from the Listening passage:

> '*Although* there are many pressures on us to restrain this drive, we all behave aggressively to some extent at some time or other.'
> 'Some of these rules are formal, *while* others are informal . . .'
> 'Managers tend to believe that management is their right *whereas* non-managers tend to think that managers should be more open to questioning and criticism.'

Now rewrite the following sentences using the construction or language given in brackets. The first one has been done for you.

1. Although we all have in us an aggressive impulse, there are many pressures on us to restrain it. (sentence connector)
   We all have in us an aggressive impulse. However, there are many pressures on us to restrain it.
2. Some of the outlets for our aggression are external; others, however, are within our direct experience. (subordinate clause)
3. There is a divergence of interests between managers and non-managers. (differ)
4. Managers are more interested than non-managers in achieving efficiency, economy and productivity. (non-managers . . . not as interested)
5. The values of managers and non-managers do not match at all. (the same)
6. Although there are negative aspects of conflict, it is not a bad thing. (phrase of contrast)
7. Although conflict can lead to tension, it can also bring real benefits. (sentence connector)
8. Some rules in an organisation are formal and written, but others are informal and unwritten. (subordinate clause)
9. Change is important; however, change itself can be good or bad. (phrase of contrast)
10. Organisations which actively try to resolve conflicts are generally healthy if we compare them with those that ignore conflicts. (in comparison)

4.2   Toning down information (see Unit 70 in *Language Reference for Business English*)

Look at the following sentences taken from the Listening passage:

'Managers *tend to* believe that management is their right . . .'
'We all behave aggressively *to some extent* . . .'
'The conclusion you *might* draw is that conflict is a bad thing . . .'

Now tone down the following sentences using the language techniques given in brackets. The first one has been done for you.

1. We all have in us an aggressive instinct. (seem)
   We all seem to have in us an aggressive instinct.
   It seems (that) we all have in us an aggressive instinct.
2. There are many pressures on us to restrain this drive. (way)
3. We are going to spend a little time on discussing the causes of conflict. (just)
4. Our industry doesn't have bad industrial relations. (tend)
5. We should consider conflict as a positive force. (maybe)
6. Conflict has brought some real advantages. (appear)
7. Conflict is one of the ways of changing the rules. (extent)
8. Conflict wastes time and energy. (inclined)
9. Conflict taxes some people (a little), while others become stimulated. (appear)
10. During conflicts communication is impaired. (tend)
11. This will lead to greater hostility between the parties. (perhaps)
12. So that was an introduction to the session. (just)

5   Word study

Group the following list of fifteen words into five categories, with three words with associated meanings in each.

problem	conflict	govern	drive	status
drawback	urge	rule	aggression	position
procedure	impulse	disadvantage	clash	level

6   Transfer

You are the employee relations manager at Codix. One of your junior managers is bad at handling the industrial side of his activities. Each time there is the slightest disagreement or conflict he comes and asks you to sort it out. Write a memo to him explaining the role of conflict and assuring him of its positive sides.

Section B: Employee health, safety and welfare

There is always a conflict between the needs of the employer to push for increased output and efficiency, and the needs of the employee to be protected from the hazards of the work-place. In the mid-nineteenth century these tensions centred almost entirely on the long hours and heavy physical demands. In the closing years of the twentieth century the tensions are more varied and more subtle, but concern about them remains as great.

Part 1: The scope and importance of health, safety and welfare

1 Warm-up

1.1   Employee health, safety and welfare is a matter of concern for various groups and individuals. To whom is it a concern?

1.2   One authority has claimed that there are three causes of accidents. What are they?

2 Reading

As you read, complete Charts 8.3 and 8.4.

THE SCOPE OF HEALTH, SAFETY AND WELFARE

The dictionary defines welfare as 'well-being'; so health and safety are strictly aspects of employee welfare, which have been separately identified. Various authors have provided wide definitions for welfare, encompassing not only the early concerns with workers' physical working conditions – sanitation, canteens, hours of work, rest pauses, etc. – but also the 'human relations school of thought', due to the achievement of job satisfaction being seen as a way to bring about higher productivity.

There are two primary areas of benefit to the individual from the provision of welfare facilities: physical benefits and emotional/psychological benefits. Physical benefits stem primarily from measures to improve health and safety, as well as from the provision of paid holidays, reduced working hours and such like. Emotional welfare stems chiefly from any provisions made to improve mental health, for example counselling, improved communications, or anything involving the 'human relations' needs of people at work. These benefits are, however, highly inter-related and most welfare activities would potentially have both physical and emotional benefits.

Many provisions are less clearly seen as welfare when, for example, they are long-standing provisions made by many employers, such as canteens and time off for doctor's appointments. Other provisions are less clearly seen as welfare when they are enshrined in the contract of employment and therefore seen as standard. Holiday entitlement would come into this group: however, the amount of holiday is far from standard. In the United Kingdom, holiday entitlement generally ranges from three to six weeks per year, which compares very favourably with the two weeks to which many American employees are entitled.

Chart 8.3 Welfare areas and benefits

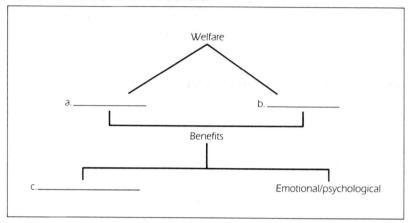

THE IMPORTANCE OF HEALTH, SAFETY AND WELFARE

The importance of health, safety and welfare from the employees' point of view is clear – their lives and futures are at risk. Health and safety have been given increasing emphasis by the trade unions, especially from the late sixties. Eva and Oswald (1981), in their book on the trade union approach to health and safety, identify a number of union concerns in the early seventies, which included:

1. Despite the health and safety laws, the number of accidents continued to rise.
2. New technologies were continually being introduced that created new hazards not covered by existing laws.
3. New diseases caused by working conditions began to be detected.
4. Over six million workers in the rapidly growing welfare and state sectors (like schools, hospitals and government services) were not covered by any legislation.
5. The early seventies was a period of pay restraint and the unions were keener at this time to get involved in health and safety.

From the point of view of the employer there are a variety of reasons for supporting health, safety and welfare provision, apart from their legal obligations. It would be unfair to say that altruism does not play a part in employers' motives for improving these provisions, but there are other major influencing factors. The number of working days lost due to accidents at work was 10½ million in the year 1981/2. If this figure were reduced by only a small percentage, the employer would save a considerable amount of money and trouble. One of the side effects of employees with personal problems is that the quality of their work is often affected.

There is also a general feeling that employees whose health, safety and welfare are well looked after by the employer will be more productive and loyal employees and may cause fewer industrial relations problems, as indicated by the following quote from a personnel director: 'It is very difficult for people who have been treated well to take a militant attitude to 1 per cent one way or the other on a pay deal.'

However, there is continual conflict between health, safety and welfare considerations and other business priorities, especially in times of recession when production considerations consistently tend to outweigh health and safety matters as a priority in management calculations.

Chart 8.4   Reasons for the importance of health, safety and welfare

To the employee: 1. Lives _____ at risk

To trade unions: 1. Rise _____

2. Hazards of _____

3. New _____

4. Over six million workers _____

_____ by any legislation

To employer: 1. Altruism

2. _____

3. _____ of employees

4. Fewer _____ problems

3   Comprehension/interpretation

3.1   What were the earlier concerns about workers' physical conditions?
3.2   What welfare provisions can provide emotional benefits to the workers?
3.3   Why are holidays less clearly a welfare consideration?
3.4   What typically happens to welfare concerns in times of recession?

4 Language focus

4.1   Subordinate clauses (see Unit 36 in *Language Reference for Business English*)

Look at the following sentences taken from the Reading passage:

'It is very difficult for people *who have been treated well* to take a militant attitude . . .'
'*If this figure were reduced by only a small percentage* the employer would save a considerable amount of money and trouble.'

Now rewrite the following sentences using a subordinate clause of the type shown in brackets. The first one has been done for you.

1. The dictionary defines welfare as 'well-being'; so health and safety are strictly aspects of employee welfare. (cause)
   As the dictionary defines welfare as 'well-being', health and safety are strictly aspects of employee welfare.
2. Various authors have provided definitions. The definitions cover both physical working conditions and human relations. (relative)
3. Early authors wrote about workers' physical working conditions. They included sanitation, canteens, hours of work, and rest pauses. (verb . . . *ing*)
4. Early authors also developed the 'human relations school of thought', due to the achievement of job satisfaction being seen as a way to bring about higher productivity. (cause)
5. There are two primary areas of benefit to the individual from the provision of welfare facilities. We identify them as physical benefits and emotional/ psychological benefits. (verb . . . *ed*)
6. Companies improved health and safety; then the workers' physical condition would improve too. (condition)
7. Despite the introduction of health and safety laws, the number of accidents has continued to rise. (contrast)
8. New diseases can be detected. Working conditions cause them. (relative)
9. Employers support health, safety and welfare provisions. The objective is to improve workers' performance. (purpose)
10. One director asked, 'Why have the workers taken industrial action when we look after them so well?'

4.2 Addition (see Unit 60 in *Language Reference for Business English*)

Look at the following sentences taken from the Reading passage:

'There is *also* a general feeling that employees whose health, safety and welfare are well looked after by the employer will be more productive.'
'Various authors have provided wide definitions for welfare, encompassing *not only* the early concerns with workers' physical working conditions – sanitation, canteens, hours of work, rest pauses, etc. – *but also* the "human relations school of thought".'
'Physical benefits stem primarily from measures to improve health and safety, *as well as* from the provision of paid holidays, reduced working hours and such like.'
'Most welfare activities would potentially have *both* physical *and* emotional benefits.'

Are the following sentences right or wrong? If wrong, make the necessary correction.

1. Health and safety are the both aspects of employee welfare.
2. Welfare covers not only sanitation but also canteens, hours of work and rest pauses.
3. As well as provide physical benefits, welfare also provides emotional/psychological benefits.
4. Emotional welfare provisions aim to improve mental health. Too they involve the 'human relations' needs of people at work.
5. The importance of health, safety and welfare is clear from the employees' point of view. Also the trade unions have given it increasing emphasis.

Now link each sentence part on the left with its appropriate other part on the right:

1. According to Maslow's hierarchy of human needs, employees need both safety	a. workers also need to be loved.
	b. they need it in the workplace, too.
	c. and freedom from fear and threat.
2. Modern organisations try to meet not only physiological needs	d. in addition, they will not respond to higher-level opportunities.
3. In addition to belonging,	e. but also security needs.
4. Security needs must be satisfied at home	f. as well as in the workplace.
5. People need affection at home;	
6. If security needs are not met, workers will get frustrated;	

5 Word study

Complete the following table. If necessary, use your dictionary.

Noun	Adjective	Opposite adjective
health	_____	_____
_____	safe	_____
width	_____	narrow
_____	high	_____
_____	reduced	_____
law	_____	_____
_____	separate	_____
satisfaction	_____	unsatisfactory
generality	_____	_____
_____	decreasing/ declining	growing

6 Transfer

Discuss what measures your organisation can take to prevent accidents. In the US, the National Safety Council says that accident prevention depends on the three E's: engineering, education and enforcement. What can be done in your workplace?

Part 2: When to report an accident

1 Warm-up

1.1 Who is responsible for safety at work?
1.2 Management is obliged to provide safety training to the employees. What are the three purposes of safety training?

2 Listening

Codix has a safety officer whose responsibilities include safety training to ensure the health and safety of Codix employees at work. In this extract he is instructing three plant supervisors on what to do in the case of an accident. As you listen, complete Chart 8.5.

Chart 8.5 What accidents must be reported under the Occupational Safety and Health Act (OHSA)

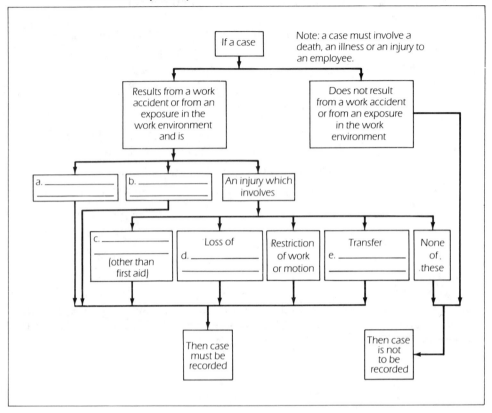

3   Comprehension/interpretation

3.1   What is every employer in the UK required to prepare?

3.2   What role does the safety officer perform?

3.3   What types of injury or illness are not connected to work?

3.4   What types of illness must be reported?

4 Language focus

4.1 **Like** versus **as** (see Unit 65 in *Language Reference for Business English*)

Look at the following sentences taken from the Listening passage:

> '*As* you know, every employer in this country is required by law to prepare a written statement *like* this.'
> 'My role as safety officer is to act *as* a kind of inhouse factory inspector . . .'

Now complete the following sentences with either **like** or **as**:

1. _____ you've all seen this safety report before, we needn't spend much time on it.
2. _____ safety officer, my job is to ensure that cases _____ accidents and injuries are reported.
3. The steps to be taken after an accident are _____ follows.
4. The first question is, 'Does it look _____ a serious accident?'
5. Such places _____ the washrooms and the canteen all constitute the work-place.
6. Accidents involving medical assistance _____ first aid needn't be recorded.
7. Some of you have been trained _____ first-aid officers.
8. _____ usual, there will always be exceptions to the rule.
9. If a person can't carry out their work _____ before, then the accident needs reporting.
10. _____ a precaution, whenever you are in doubt report the accident.

4.2 Question types (see Skill 2 in *Language Reference for Business English*)

Look at the following sentences taken from the Listening passage:

> '*First of all, when is an accident within the scope of the provisions?*' (factual)
> '*Does that mean that we don't need to report or record any cases which don't happen at work?*' (closed)
> '*Now that's fairly broad, isn't it?*' (leading)

Now classify the following questions according to type:

1. I suppose you have all seen this document before?
2. Have you seen this document before?
3. What constitutes an accident in the workplace?
4. Could you give me an example of an accident at work?
5. How do you react to those who say that workplace accidents are increasing?
6. Don't you agree that some people are just accident-prone?
7. So you agree that we should improve our safety precautions?
8. Do you think we can improve our safety record?
9. A: How do you think we can improve our safety record?
   B: Good question. Well, what do you think?
10. Do you think that now is the right time to invest in safety?

5 Word study

Complete the following word table.

Noun	Adjective
death	_____
_____	sick
_____	injured
health	_____
safety	_____
accident	_____
_____	official
_____	responsible
_____	required
_____	limited
_____	provided
_____	connected

6 Transfer

Draft a health and safety policy for your organisation. Include information about:

- general policy on health and safety, and
- specific hazards and how they are to be dealt with.

KEY

UNIT 1
The role of personnel management

Section A: What is personnel management?

Part 1: Key aspects of personnel management

1 Warm-up

1.1 To get results through people.
1.2 Recruitment, safety, training and labour relations.

2 Reading

In Chart 1.1:

a.	Line	e.	Line
b.	Staff	f.	Line
c.	Staff	g.	Staff
d.	Staff		

3 Comprehension/interpretation

3.1 Personnel management is directed mainly at the organisation's employees; human resources management at management needs for human resources (not necessarily employees).
3.2 Recruiting, interviewing, selecting and training.
3.3 A line function, a co-ordinative function and a staff function.
3.4 A line function to own department; a co-ordinative function to the top executive; staff functions to line management.

4 Language focus

4.1 Present passive verb forms

2. At present the organisation's manpower needs are being assessed.
3. All managers can be considered as personnel managers.
4. Next week a seminar on delegation is being offered.
5. The new appraisal scheme is still being considered by the MD. It is expected to be introduced/We expect it to be introduced later this year.
6. Orienting, training and working to improve job performance are included in the personnel manager's responsibilities.
7. The personnel manager will be being advised by the line managers during the evaluation.
8. In small organisations, personnel duties may be carried out by line managers unassisted.

1. John expected to be asked/consulted about the new appraisal scheme.
2. By being involved, John hoped to make his own contribution.
3. While being consulted, John hoped to make his own contribution.
4. He said, 'Let the questions be raised now rather than later.'
5. After being made redundant, John received many letters of support.

4.2 Like versus as

1.	as	5.	like
2.	like	6.	as
3.	As	7.	like
4.	as	8.	like

5 Word study

Verb	Noun
orient	orientation
perform	performance
analyse	analysis
benefit	benefit
evaluate	evaluation
appraise	appraisal
develop	development
compensate	compensation
promote	promotion

6 Transfer

Suggested points for discussion:

- To hire the wrong person for the job.
- Your people not doing their best.
- High turnover.
- To waste time with useless interviews.
- To have your company taken to court because of your discriminatory actions.
- To have some of your employees think their salaries are unfair and inequitable relative to others in the organisation.
- A lack of training undermining your department's effectiveness.
- To commit any unfair labour practices.

Part 2: Introducing the personnel team

1 Warm-up

1.1 Personnel manager
Personnel officer for training and development
Personnel officer for health, safety and welfare
Personnel officer for administration
Personnel assistant for remuneration

1.2 Personnel director
Employee relations manager
Training and development manager
Payment manager
Employment manager
Personnel administration manager

Listening tapescript

A: Okay, Paul, I'd like to take this opportunity of welcoming you to Codix. And for those of you who weren't at the last meeting, I'd like to introduce Paul Bailey.

B: Thank you.

A: What Paul and I planned for this meeting is, first of all, just to run through the structure of the department.

All: Okay. Fine.

A: Then, Paul, if you have any general questions, we can handle them straight away.

B: Fine.

A: Right, well, let's get started then. As you can see, the department is headed by me as personnel director. I act as the main spokesman of the department and represent personnel issues in all our senior management discussions and also in policy-making meetings. Then there are four managers who report to me, though one of the positions is vacant at present. Let's take them individually. First there is our recruitment and selection manager. She is responsible for maintaining contact within the community – looking for manpower according to our needs. In fact, she now has to travel extensively to search for qualified job applicants – that's a feature of the job market at present. Next we have the compensation and benefits manager. He handles the company's employee benefits programme, that's primarily health insurance and pension plans. Then we have our training and development manager. This post is currently vacant but we are advertising in the national press as well using other channels: so we hope to have someone installed pretty soon. I would like to say that this position, training and development manager, is crucial to our thinking at Codix. We have a strong tradition of providing vocational training for our people and a sizable team of specialists in charge of planning, organising and directing a wide range of training activities. But I'll come back the team a bit later. Finally there's our employee relations manager. She deals with the collective relationship between management and employees and advises us, that is the organisation, on all aspects of union–management relations. So those are the four managers who are accountable to me; and each manager takes care of a section.
  So moving on. Each of these managers is supported by an individual or a small

team. In recruitment and selection the manager is assisted by what we call a recruitment officer. The compensation and benefits manager works with a benefits administrator and a job analyst in a small team. Our training and development manager is supported by two training officers, and they are in charge of a team of some seven instructors. And finally there is our employee relations manager who is supported by two employee relations officers. Of course, I've forgotten to mention our health, safety and welfare people. They are, naturally, part of the management team, but not part of the personnel department. They provide staff or service functions to the whole organisation. Firstly there's the medical officer, who is, in fact, a trained doctor. Then there is the safety officer, who has two broad activities – to make our work safe and to ensure safe working practices throughout the organisation. And last the two occupational nurses who also deal directly with working safely and safety training. So that's the personnel department, the sections and the teams, together with the support of the health, safety and welfare people.

B: Right. Thank you.

2 Listening

In Chart 1.2:

a.	Recruitment and selection	e.	Occupational health nurses
b.	Training and development	f.	Benefits administrator
c.	Employee relations	g.	Job analyst
d.	Safety officer	h.	Instructors

3 Comprehension/interpretation

3.1   She is responsible for maintaining contact within the community.
3.2   Health insurance and pension plans.
3.3   Planning, organising and directing a wide range of training activities.
3.4   To make the work safe and to ensure safe working practices throughout the organisation.

4 Language focus

4.1   Describing the organisation

1. The personnel director reports to the president.
2. The personnel director is responsible for developing personnel policy for the company.
3. As you can see from the chart, the personnel department is divided into four sections.
4. The personnel director is supported by four section leaders, who are all managers.
5. Also under the personnel director are the medical officer, the safety officer and the nurses.
6. Each manager is in charge of one of the following specialist areas: recruitment, compensation, training and employee relations.
7. The compensation and benefits manager is supported/assisted by a small team.
8. The benefits administrator reports to the compensation and benefits manager.
9. In addition to the parent company, Codix is at present planning to open a subsidiary in the north-east of England.
10. The present personnel director will also take care of/be in charge of personnel policy in the new company.

4.2   Connecting and sequencing ideas

1. first (of all)
2. the second stage
3. After
4. finally
5. Having
6. first(ly)
7. second(ly)
8. third(ly)
9. lastly/finally
10. The final
11. before
12. first
13. first(ly)
14. before

5   Word study

Verb	Noun concept	Noun person
apply	application	applicant
instruct	instruction	instructor
represent	representation	representative
pension off	pension	pensioner
provide	provision	provider
specialise	specialisation	specialist
	speciality (Br.E.)	
	specialty (Am.E.)	
organise	organisation	organiser
advise	advice	adviser/advisor

Section B: Personnel management philosophy

Part 1: Developing your personnel management philosophy

1   Warm-up

1.1   Experiences, education and background.
1.2   New knowledge and experiences.

2   Reading

In Chart 1.4:

1. Y
2. X
3. Y
4. Y
5. X
6. Y
7. Y
8. X

In Chart 1.5:

1. I
2. IV
3. I
4. IV
5. IV
6. IV
7. I
8. IV
9. I

3 Comprehension/interpretation

3.1 Top management's personnel philosophy and the basic assumptions you make about people.

3.2 A top-level personnel policy committee.

3.3 Organisations

3.4 A shift from blue-collar to white-collar workers.

4 Language focus

4.1 Present simple versus present continuous

1. Theory X states that workers cannot be trusted to work.
2. At present the personnel policy committee consists of our top officers – which shows our commitment to our employees.
3. If we look at the statistics, we can see that workers are becoming better-educated and more concerned with their lifestyles.
4. At present we are working on a policy to give everyone a personal opportunity for self-fulfilment.
5. Our employees definitely feel that they belong in this organisation.
6. The problem of redundancies is hardly ever discussed here.
7. A: Have you got the appraisal forms?
   B: Not yet. They are still being typed up.
8. A: Any new developments?
   B: Yes, we are just running a series of seminars on quality management.
9. I'm sorry but I don't agree with the new personnel policy.
10. Just look at what is happening in the service sector!

4.2 Be

1. there was
2. there is
3. there is
4. it is
5. there has not been . . . it is
6. It is
7. there will be . . . they are
8. there is
9. There is . . . it is
10. It is
11. it is
12. it is

5 Word study

1. d   2. g   3. f   4. j   5. h   6. a   7. i   8. b   9. e   10. c

Part 2: Motivation – a central issue?

1 Warm-up

1.2 Variety, autonomy, responsibility, challenge, interaction, task significance, goals and feedback.

Listening tapescript

Good evening, everybody. It's just gone eight and so I'd like to welcome you all to our round-table discussion. The subject of this evening's meeting is motivation, and I am pleased to see that so many of you were motivated to come. I'm also delighted to welcome our panel, who come from a variety of local firms. I'm sure their faces are familiar to most of you. In any case, in a moment I'll ask them to introduce themselves to you.

My name is Philip Bradshaw and I'm personnel director at Codix. I am also privileged to be chairman of the northern branch of the APM. For this evening's meeting I would like to suggest that we have a contribution from each panelist followed by comments and questions from the audience. We will divide the evening into two sessions of roughly one hour each, with a break for half an hour at around 9 o'clock. That means we will end at 10.30 or thereabouts. I hope that covers the basic administration.

So, on to this evening's theme: motivation. Much has been written, and even more spoken, about this subject. On one thing I think we would all agree: motivating employees is a major concern of managers. And it's easy to see why. If you can't motivate your employees to get their jobs done, you are destined to fail as manager.

The question of how to motivate someone is a complex one, and one for which there are no quick answers. You are bound to have all done your reading of the authorities – Maslow and Alderfer, Herzberg and Vroom. And if you haven't, you certainly should have. Yet one 'law' of motivation seems to apply quite consistently, and that is: *People are usually motivated or driven to behave in a way that they feel leads to rewards*. In other words, as a rough-and-ready rule, motivating someone requires two things. First, find out what the person wants and hold it out as a possible reward. And second, make sure that he or she feels that effort on his or her part will probably lead to obtaining that reward. One without the other won't work. Let me give you an example. Telling one of your sales team managers that you'll definitely make her sales manager if her monthly sales hit £250,000 won't motivate her – even if she *wants* to be sales manager – unless she also thinks there is a reasonable chance, unless she thinks it is likely that she can, in fact, make sales of £250,000. So, my point is, both *desire* and *ability* are required. People are motivated to accomplish those tasks that they feel will definitely or are likely to lead to rewards. This is the essence of motivation. And, of course, this idea has important implications for all your personnel activities. Each personnel management activity contributes to your workers' motivation.

Let's take a look at the question of ability. Your first task is to ask yourself the question, 'Could my employee do the job if he or she wanted to?' And there are several personnel management things you can do to help ensure that the answer is yes. First, analyse the job. Determine the skill requirements. Develop job descriptions. Second, carry out the selection. Make sure you hire people with the aptitude and potential to do the job. Third, orient and train these people. Ensure that you provide them with the basic skills they need to carry out their jobs. So, if you've done everything right up to this point, you can be fairly sure that subordinates will feel they are capable of accomplishing their tasks; in other words, that they have the *ability* to do so. So that was my first point about ability.

What about desire? Just as you asked yourself the question about ability. you have to ask yourself about desire: 'Is the reward important to the employees – do they have the *desire* to do the job?' This is my second point: our second requirement for motivating someone, and it involves some of our most important personnel management activities. Here again there are vital steps we can take to ensure that our employees have the desire to do the job. For example, look at the wages and salaries you pay employees: their financial incentives. Look at the nonfinancial incentives – the benefits and services that the company provides.

Now, if you've done an effective job in your personnel management activities (and I'm positive most of you have) your employees should be motivated and performance should be high. Your next step is *to appraise performance*. And here you should ask yourself: 'Did motivation take place?' and 'If not, why not?' If the answer is no, you have to identify the problem. Perhaps you should reorganise. You may need a change in selection standards. You might need to provide more training. Etc., etc. In other words, you *identify the problem* (if you have one) and *take corrective action*.

Well, I see from my watch that it's nearly ten past eight. I am sure our panelists this evening are going to address these and other issues, and so at this point it gives me great pleasure . . .

2   Listening

In Chart 1.6:

a. ability
b. Carry out selection
c. Orient and train
d. Look at the wages and salaries
e. Look at the non-financial benefits
f. Identify the problem
g. Take corrective action

3   Comprehension/interpretation

3.1   Motivation derives from *ability* to achieve the target and desire for the *reward*.
3,2   Aptitude and potential.
3.3   Benefits and services.
3.4   Reorganise
       Change the selection standards
       Provide more training

4 Language focus

4.1 Scale of likelihood

2. I am sure/certain/positive that these policies will affect the desire of employees to stay or leave.
   These policies are certain/positive/bound to affect the desire of employees to stay or leave.
   These policies will definitely/certainly affect the desire of employees to stay or leave.
3. Our culture may/might enhance or decrease an individual's performance.
4. I am sure/certain/positive that a creative, unconventional person won't fit into this culture.
   A creative, unconventional person certainly/definitely won't fit into this culture.
   A creative, unconventional person can't (possibly) fit into this culture.
5. Our type of culture is likely to motivate certain types of individual.
   It is likely that our type of culture will motivate certain types of individual.
6. Our pension plans may/might attract some of our employees.
7. Employees are unlikely to have lifetime loyalty to this company.
   It is unlikely that employees will have lifetime loyalty to this company.
8. I am sure/certain/positive that the changes in working climate have an effect on the employees.
   The changes in working climate are sure/certain/bound to have an effect on the employees.
   The changes in working climate will definitely/certainly have an effect on the employees.
9. Employees are likely to expect the management to improve benefits.
   It is likely that employees will expect the management to improve benefits.
10. I am sure/certain/positive that we won't reward all individuals equally.
    We certainly/definitely won't reward all individuals equally.
    We can't (possibly) reward all individuals equally.

4.2 Expressions of clock time

1. *Wrong:* half an hour
2. *Wrong:* an hour and a half/one and a half hours
3. *Am.E. right*
   Br.E. wrong: at 3 o'cock
4. *Wrong:* at half past three
5. *Right*
6. *Wrong:* three minutes past nine
7. *Right*
8. *Wrong:* seven p.m. or seven o'clock (in the evening)
9. *Right*
10. *Right*

5   Word study

Noun	Adjective
variety	various
contribution	contributory
administration	administrative
possibility	possible
example	exemplary
ability	able
essence	essential
importance	important
basis	basic
finance	financial
correction	corrective
action	active

UNIT 2
Job analysis

Section A: The nature of and steps in job analysis

Part 1: The six steps in job analysis

1 Warm-up

1.1   An organisation chart is a 'snapshot' of a department at a particular point of time and shows:

- titles of each manager's job,
- who is accountable to whom, and
- who is in charge of what department.

A job analysis shows:

- the duties and natures of the jobs, and
- the kinds of people (in terms of skills and experience) who should be hired for them.

1.2   Recruitment and selection
Compensation
Performance appraisal
Training

2 Reading

Step 1. Determine the use of job analysis information
Step 2. Collect background information
Step 3. Select representative positions to be analysed
Step 4. Collect job analysis information
Step 5. Review the information with the participants
Step 6. Develop a job description and a job specification

In Chart 2.1:

a.   plant managers
b.   suppliers
c.   Information
d.   plant managers
e.   Inventory
f.   plant managers

3 Comprehension/interpretation

3.1 Interviewing the employee.
3.2 Organisation chart.
3.3 The worker performing the job and the worker's immediate supervisor.
3.4 Personal qualities, traits, skills and backgrounds required for getting the job done.

4 Language focus

4.1 Verb . . . *ing*

1. recruiting/hiring
2. analysing
3. writing
4. showing/defining/identifying
5. Preparing/Developing
6. identifying/defining/showing
7. hiring/recruiting
8. training
9. supervising
10. administering
11. developing/preparing
12. defining/showing

4.2 Indirect questions

2. The organisation chart showed how the job fitted into the overall organisation.
3. The process chart showed how the work had flowed.
4. The process chart shows who has been receiving inventory from the suppliers.
5. The existing job description showed what other information we needed.
6. The written job description will show what the activities and responsibilities of the job are.
7. The person specification identified what qualities, skills and backgrounds the applicant had to have.
8. Our sales manager decided last week when the recruitment would take place.
9. The sales manager wanted to know if we had completed the job analysis.
10. The sales manager asked why it was taking so long to analyse all the data.

5 Word study

1. e   2. j   3. g   4. h   5. l   6. d   7. a   8. c   9. k   10. f   11. o   12. m
13. b   14. i   15. n

Part 2: Collecting job analysis information

1 Warm-up

1.1 Interview

1.2 Questionnaire

Listening tapescript

JA: Oh, Arthur, come in and take a seat.

AB: Thanks.

JA: Well, as you know we are carrying out a series of interviews to collect information about the supervisors' jobs.

AB: Yes, I know about the interviews and the purpose, and I must say that I'm not too impressed about the regrading suggestion.

JA: Well, I think we'd better leave the question of regrading to another meeting, if that's okay with you?

AB: Oh. All right, fine. So you want to ask me some questions?

JA: Yes, Arthur. You've already filled in the questionnaire, but as you probably realise it couldn't ask all the questions. So that's where this interview fits in – to complete the picture. Okay?

AB: Yes, fine.

JA: It'll take about half an hour.

AB: Right.

JA: So, I've got some questions here and I'm going to make some notes during the interview. You'll have a chance to look at my notes afterwards. Is that okay?

AB: Yes, fine.

JA: Right. So, what exactly is your job title?

AB: Production supervisor . . . in the packaging department.

JA: And how long have you been in that job?

AB: Well, let me see. I started at Codix seven years ago, and I've been a supervisor for three years now.

JA: And what are the major duties?

AB: Well, firstly to ensure that our packaging work meets with the requirements. For that we need to have the equipment operating properly.

JA: What exactly do you mean?

AB: Well, if one part of the equipment isn't working properly, then it should be reported to me, and I report it to the plant manager.

JA: So, to monitor the equipment. What else?

AB: I'm also in charge of the packaging team. I instruct them about what to do. Then I assign different tasks to them on the packaging line, and of course I review their work – to ensure it meets the specifications.

JA: So, let me just go over those points again. Firstly, it's your job to instruct the packaging team about what to do.

AB: Yes, that's right.

JA: Then you also have to assign different tasks to them – where they are to work on the line.

AB: Yes.

JA: And then you're also responsible for reviewing their work – to ensure it meets the specifications.

AB: Yes, that's about it.

JA: And if it doesn't?

AB: And if it doesn't what?

JA: Sorry, if their work doesn't meet specifications. What do you do?

AB: Then I've got to sort it out.

JA: What about accidents?

AB: Yes, any accidents must be reported to me – and I then contact the medical officer and also fill in an accident report form.

JA: And who gets these forms?

AB: Paul Munroe, the plant manager.

JA: So, you receive reports of accidents and fill in report forms?

AB: Yes, that's right.

JA: So you've got the equipment to look after, the team, and anything else?

AB: Well, there's the packaging materials, of course. I have to make sure that we've got enough at the beginning of each shift for the packaging.

JA: Fine. And where do you work?

AB: On the factory floor.

JA: Do you ever get called away?

AB: Well, occasionally to the phone or to the plant manager's office. But my people all work on the shopfloor.

JA: And who do you report to?

AB: To Paul Munroe, the plant manager.

JA: Okay, can we now look at the working conditions. What's it like on the shopfloor?

AB: Well, obviously it's quite noisy.

JA: Do you think the noise level is unreasonable?

AB: No.

JA: Can the shopfloor workers talk above the noise?

AB: Yes, if they shout.

JA: And does it get dirty?

AB: No, not if the line is working properly and we don't have any spillages.

JA: And heat? Does it get hot?

AB: No, the chocolate would all melt if it did.

JA: And what would you say are the greatest stresses and strains of the job?

AB: I suppose instructing new workers – because we've had quite a lot of new workers recently.

JA: I see.

AB: And the other thing is generally maintaining standards – checking that the work is up to requirements.

JA: And do you feel tired at the end of a shift?

AB: Oh yes.

JA: Physically or mentally?

AB: Well, I suppose it's mentally really because there are a lot of things that I need to check. I need to check . . .

2 Listening

Chart 2.2

General
Employee name: Arthur Brent
Present job title: Production Supervisor
Department: Packaging

Major duties
1. To ensure that packaging work meets with the requirements.
2. To monitor the equipment.
3. To instruct the packaging team about what to do.
4. To assign different tasks to them
5. To review their work – to ensure it meets the specifications.
6. To receive reports of accidents and fill in report forms.
7. To make sure that they've got enough packaging material at the beginning of each shift.

Place of work
Normally on shopfloor
Occasionally called to phone or to plant manager's office

Job conditions

	Acceptable	Unacceptable
Noise	✓	☐
Dirt	✓	☐
Heat	✓	☐

Demands of job
Which tasks cause particular stress?
1. Instructing new workers
2. Generally maintaining standards

---

3 Comprehension/interpretation

3.1 Regrading.
3.2 Questionnaire.
3.3 The medical officer and the plant manager.
3.4 Mentally tired.

4 Language focus

4.1 Questions

A: When did you start at Codix?
A: And how long have you been a supervisor?
A: And what exactly do you?
A: Who do you report to?
A: And how many people are there in your team?
A: What equipment do you use?
A: Does it ever break down?
A: Who repairs it?
A: Has anybody had an accident recently?
A: When did the last accident happen?

4.2 For versus during

1. during
2. for
3. during
4. for
5. during/for
6. for
7. for
8. during . . . for

5 Word study

carry	out	an interview
meet	with	the requirements
sort	out	the problem
look	at	the notes
report	to	the plant manager
look	after	the equipment
start	at	Codix

Section B: Job description and person specification

Part 1: The job description

1 Warm-up

1.1
1. Job identification
2. Context
3. Job summary
4. Job content
5. Performance standards
6. Working conditions

1.2 It should be:

- clear
- specific (appropriate level of detail)
- brief

2 Reading

In Chart 2.3:

a.	1	g.	1
b.	5	h.	2
c.	2	i.	2
d.	6	j.	4
e.	5	k.	6
f.	4	l.	3

3 Comprehension/interpretation

3.1 Job title, job code, the date of the job description, the writer and the name of the person who approved it.

3.2 Because it is not always easy to define performance objectively.

3.3 Top management.

3.4 Lower-level jobs.

4 Language focus

4.1 Cause and effect

Suggested answers:

2. Selection of managers depends on accurate assessment because managers use a wide variety of skills.
3. Different reasons may lead organisations to hire experienced managers.
4. The talent does not exist within the organisation. Therefore, the organisation may recruit from outside.
5. Because of the frequent difficulty of evaluating a manager's past performance, interviewers use other assessment tools.
6. Since potential managers haven't yet had any work experience, they are difficult to recruit.
7. Good university or college performance does not automatically lead to good managerial performance.
8. Non-academic interests can provide some insights into managerial potential. As a result, many organisations look for evidence of extra-curricular managerial interest.
9. Several managers normally interview a candidate because of the increased likelihood of making a good choice.
10. Different viewpoints reduce the risk of losing an effective manager because one interviewer is biased/has a bias.

4.2 All, each, every

day	–	all/each/every (*all the day* and *all of the day* are possible, too)
equipment	–	all/all the/all of the
machines	–	all/all the/all of the/each of the
information	–	all/all the/all of the
hour	–	each/every
employee	–	each/every
jobs	–	all/all the/all of the/each of the
work	–	all/all the/all of the (*each work* and *every work* are possible where work is countable and means an object produced by writing or painting, e.g. *a work of art*)

1. Everyone/Everybody
2. every/each
3. All
4. everything
5. each/all

5 Word study

Verbs	Nouns
specify	specification
indicate	indication
describe	description
present	presentation
state	statement
list	list
identify	identification
portray	portrayal
define	definition
summarise	summary
contain	content
include	inclusion

Part 2: Defining the human characteristics

1 Warm-up

1.1 Relevant training and length of previous service.
1.2 You need to specify qualities such as personal traits, personality, interests, etc. which would imply some potential.

Listening tapescript

SM: Well, Peter, according to my files we haven't prepared a person specification for a team leader before.

DM: No, what's happened up till now is that we've promoted the analyst/programmers to junior project leaders. But last year we got eight new analyst/programmers, so now we've got a bit of a bottleneck at junior project leader level; so we've needed to create a new category – and we've called it team leader.

SM: So this is a position between analyst programmer and junior project leader?

DM: Yes, that's right.

SM: Okay. So, Peter, you've seen one of these person specification forms before, haven't you?

DM: Yes, on various occasions. In fact, I got one before our last meeting. By the way, what's it called again?

SM: The Rodger's seven point plan. It is particularly helpful in interviews.

DM: Yes, it really is very useful for making you think systematically about an applicant. In fact, I made a few notes this morning based on the form.

SM: Good. In that case I don't need to explain it to you. Anyway I think you know pretty well what type of people you want. I'm really just here to bounce ideas off, if you need to. So, shall we get down to business?

DM: Fine.

SM: Okay. Physical make-up. How do you see this person?

DM: Well, he or she needs to look tidy.

SM: Anything about clothes?

DM: Yes, they must dress in a 'business-like' manner.

SM: Okay, I've got as essential 'tidy and dressed in a "business-like" manner'. Okay, on to attainment.

DM: The attainment details are here. One of our project leaders had a look at one of the other forms and put this down for me. And I must say I totally agree. Oh yes, I just want to add one thing. The person has to have good keyboard skills.

SM: Okay, I'll add as essential 'good keyboard skills'. Fine. Shall we move on. The next point is general intelligence.

DM: Well, we don't need a genius in that position, but let's say above average.

SM: Anything else?

DM: Yes, we mustn't have one of those slow analytical types in this job. Must be someone who's quick at solving . . . quick at understanding problems.

SM: Okay, fine. Shall we say 'above average' and then 'quick to grasp the meaning of problems'?

DM: That sounds fine.

SM: So, the next section is special aptitudes.

DM: Yes, I've got some notes on that here: 'ability to relate to people' and 'ability to form relationships quickly'.

SM: That sounds fine. I'll put that in afterwards. Next point is interests.

DM: Yes, the person has got to be interested in both computer hardware and software.

SM: Right, I'll put that down 'interested in computer hardware and software'.

DM: Okay. What's next?

SM: Disposition.

DM: Disposition . . . disposition. Difficult one that. Mustn't be too laid-back; on the other hand shouldn't be too dynamic. Perhaps careful. I mean the team leader doesn't have to solve all the department's problems – only his or her team's.

SM: But don't you need someone who's logical, too?

DM: Yes, logical, too. I suppose the best quality or qualities would be the patience to understand problems and the logic to take appropriate action – without going over the top.

SM: So, what do you suggest I put down?

DM: I think the best is simply to write down 'logic' and 'patience'.

SM: Okay. That just leaves circumstances.

DM: Yes, there's the question of Saturday work. The person doesn't need to work every Saturday, but at least two per month . . . maybe three.

SM: So the person needn't work every Saturday?

DM: Yes, that's right.

SM: Okay, in that case let's say 'circumstances that enable attendance at work some Saturdays'.

DM: Is that it?

SM: Yes. Well, thanks very much. I wish we could get them all done as fast as this.

2 Listening

Chart 2.4

Physical make-up
Essential: Tidy and dressed in a 'business-like' manner

Attainment
Preferred: 'O' level Maths   Essential: CSE Maths minimum

Preferred: *Either*
              Attendance at a programming course, in or out of school
              or
              Demonstrate some self-taught knowledge of programming

Essential: Good keyboard skills

General intelligence
Essential: Above average
              Quick to grasp the meaning of problems

Special aptitudes
Essential: Ability to relate to people
              Ability to form relationships quickly

Interests
Essential: Interested in both computer hardware and software

Disposition
Essential: Logic
              Patience

Circumstances
Essential: Circumstances that enable attendance at work some Saturdays

---

3 Comprehension/interpretation

3.1 At junior project leader level.
3.2 Team leader.
3.3 The Rodger's seven point plan.
3.4 The project leader.

4 Language focus

4.1 Obligation and requirements

2. The applicant must have a management qualification.
3. The applicant doesn't need an MBA.
4. The applicant must show good interpersonal skills.
5. The applicant mustn't be aggressive.
6. The applicant must be of above average intelligence.
7. The applicant needn't be intellectual.
8. The applicant must be able to communicate with all levels.
9. The applicant mustn't see him/herself as a typical middle manager.
10. The applicant must be interested in developing people skills.
11. The applicant doesn't need an interest in technical aspects.
12. The applicant must show a logical approach to problem-solving.
13. The applicant mustn't seem prone to stress.
14. The applicant must have a secure family life.
15. The applicant needn't live in this region.

4.2 Have, have got and get

A: Have we run the interviews for the production post yet?
B: We still haven't had/haven't got/don't have the job specification.
A: I thought I had seen it.
B: No, we got/have had the person specification, but the job description has not come back from George.
A: But he got it about a week ago, didn't he?
B: Well, in fact he got it at the beginning of the week but he has been pretty busy.
A: Really?
B: Yes, you know the new bottling machine that he got last month.
A: I have heard about it.
B: Well, apparently they are having/have got/have had a lot of problems with it. It hasn't got/doesn't have the right speed for our belts.
A: So, are they going to get a replacement?
B: I have/have got to talk to him about that now.

5 Word study

Adjective	Opposite adjective
systematic	unsystematic
essential	inessential/non-essential
helpful	unhelpful/helpless
interested	uninterested/disinterested
patient	impatient
applicable	inapplicable
agreeable	disagreeable
intelligent	unintelligent
able	unable
careful	careless
appropriate	inappropriate
logical	illogical

UNIT 3
Planning and recruiting

Section A: Forecasting personnel requirements

Part 1: Manpower planning activities

1 *Warm-up*

1.1 To maintain and improve the ability of the organisation to achieve corporate objectives through the development of strategies designed to enhance the contribution of manpower at all times in the foreseeable future. (Stainer, 1971, p. 3)

1.2 (i) To ensure that the right people with the right skills and abilities are employed at the right time.
(ii) To be aware of the way that manpower is and will be utilised, and to improve the utilisation.
(iii) To improve manpower resources and provide satisfying work.

2 *Reading*

In Chart 3.1:

a. Feedback
b. Manpower demand
c. Internal manpower supply
d. Balance and reconcile
e. External manpower supply

3 *Comprehension/interpretation*

3.1 To increase productivity.
3.2 Current supply of manpower.
3.3 Employee wastage or turnover and trends in employee movements.
3.4 Reconsider corporate objectives or manpower utilisation.

4 Language focus

4.1 Relative clauses

2. We need to select people who/that have the best potential for the job.
3. All the candidates whom/that/∅ we saw last week seem to have great potential.
   We saw some candidates last week who all seem to have great potential.
4. We have decided to appoint John Casperton, who is at present working as a factory supervisor.
5. He is going to take over next month when Paul retires.
6. All (of) the placements that/∅ we have made have been a success.
7. Training room 101, where you intend to run the quality seminar, is much too small.
8. The training plan, which has now been published, took four weeks to prepare.
9. We are going to send Peter back to college, where he hopes to get a management qualification.
10. Our managing director, whose views on personnel you know well, has proposed a personnel planning committee.

4.2 Adjectives versus adverbs

1. accurately		7. particularly	
2. significantly		8. Clearly	
3. major		9. sensible	
4. various		10. real	
5. directly		11. lively	
6. hard		12. Eventually	

5 Word study

1. d   2. g   3. j   4. h   5. a   6. i   7. c   8. b   9. f   10. e

Part 2: Analysing staff turnover

1 Warm-up

1.1

- Retirement
- Resignation due to:
    change in company's working conditions
    opening of other workplaces in the area
    transport developments and travel-to-work patterns

1.2   On the one hand, wastage helps to get rid of 'dead wood' from the organisation; on the other, it enables 'new blood' to enter the organisation.

Listening tapescript

SM: So, the next point on the agenda is the turnover in the staff canteen. I've asked Bryan Lamb, the canteen manager, to come over at 10.30 for this part of the meeting. So he should be here any minute. He would like to go into the problem of staff turnover in . . .

CM: Good morning everyone.

All: Good morning.

SM: Well, Bryan, you're just on cue. I had just mentioned the problem of staff turnover that you wanted to discuss. So would you like to give us the background?

CM: Thanks Sandra. Well, it's a major headache. I've got two more people leaving on Friday, and I've heard that three more are going to hand in their notice in May. So, in short, we're having problems coping. Anyway, as you all know, the staff canteen has been under pressure for some time now. The growth of the organisation has led to a considerable increase in demand for hot lunches and we have been stretched to capacity. The problem has been aggravated by the high staff turnover in the kitchens over the last two years. And I'd now like to look at ways of coping better with the manpower requirements.

SM: Could you just go over the job grades in the canteen?

CM: Yes. Firstly we've got the chefs, then the serving staff, and then the clearing staff.

SM: Okay, that's clear. So, I think as a starting point it would be useful if we could make an analysis of staff turnover. We have a number of statistical techniques which will give us an indication of the scale of the problem. I've written them up on the flipchart over here for this session. So what I suggest is that we go through these. I'll explain as we go along, if you can provide the relevant figures.

CM: Okay.

SM: Right. The first one is called the annual labour turnover index; it's the simplest formula for calculating wastage as a percentage of the average number of people holding a particular job during the year. So on the top line we've got the leavers in the year, say 1990, and this figure is divided by the average number of staff in the post during that same year. Then we multiply this figure by 100 to give us a percentage – and that's the percentage wastage rate.

CM: May I suggest that we just look at the serving staff and the clearing staff?

SM: Fine.

CM: Serving staff . . . let me see. Right, last year we had 15 leavers during the year out of 48 average in the post.

SM: So, that's 15 divided by 48 as a per cent equals 31.25 per cent.

CM: But that's tremendously high. It means that almost a third of the staff left during the year.

SM: Well, yes and no. I should say at this point that this method is a little suspect because it doesn't take into account length of service, nor does it show how many left at the time of induction. So the picture may appear a little distorted. What I'd like to do is to use another calculation in a moment. But first, let's use the same calculation for the clearing staff.

CM: Just a moment . . . that's in this file. Okay. The figures for the clearing staff for last year. During the year we employed an average of 65; and leavers . . . let me see. Yes, 22 left during the year.

SM: Okay, that gives us 22 over 65 as a per cent is 33.846 per cent. Right, so that's one way of looking at the problem. I'd like to take another technique and see what results that gives us. Now, this one is called . . . the stability index. As its name implies, it is based on the number of people who could have stayed throughout the period – so we're only looking at people who could have stayed for the full year.

CM: Right. So we want the number of serving staff who were employed on 31 December . . .

SM: . . . who had been there for the full year.

CM: Oh, I see. Right . . . hang on a moment. That's 38, I think. Let me just check again. Yes, 38.

SM: And now, can you tell me how many serving staff you had on 31 December the previous year.

CM: That's . . . 46.

SM: Okay. Let's do the calculation: 38 divided by 46 as a per cent gives us 82.6 per cent. So that's your stability index for the serving staff.

CM: But that seems relatively high, doesn't it?

SM: Yes. I'll explain in a minute.

CM: So now we want to do the same calculation for the clearing staff. Right. Employed on 31 December . . . with one year's service . . . 38.

SM: Fine. And now the previous year's figure?

CM: That's 58.

SM: Okay, that gives us 38 divided by 58 as a percentage . . . 65.517 per cent. Okay, in brief, what that means is that for the serving staff . . .

2 Listening

Chart 3.2

Annual labour turnover index

Serving staff	Clearing staff
$\frac{15}{48} \times 100 = 31.25\%$	$\frac{22}{65} \times 100 = 33.846\%$

Stability index

Serving staff	Clearing staff
$\frac{38}{46} \times 100 = 82.6\%$	$\frac{38}{58} \times 100 = 65.517\%$

Chart 3.3

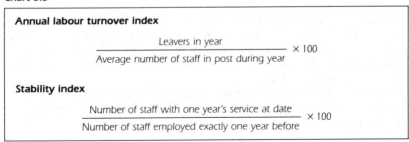

Annual labour turnover index

$$\frac{\text{Leavers in year}}{\text{Average number of staff in post during year}} \times 100$$

Stability index

$$\frac{\text{Number of staff with one year's service at date}}{\text{Number of staff employed exactly one year before}} \times 100$$

3 Comprehension/interpretation

3.1 Growth of the organisation has led to increase in demand for hot lunches, aggravated by high staff turnover in the kitchens.
3.2 Chefs, serving staff and clearing staff.
3.3 Length of service and numbers leaving at the time of induction.
3.4 The number of people who could have stayed throughout the period.

4 Language focus

4.1 Present perfect versus past simple

1. has been
2. has been aggravated
3. left
4. have handed in
5. did . . . start
6. did . . . have
7. have retired
8. recently took over/have recently taken over
9. have always felt
10. have . . . talked; noticed

4.2 Prepositions of time

1. for
2. at the end of last week/last Friday/on Friday of last week/at the end of May
3. on Wednesday of this week
4. at the end of the/this month
5. next/on
6. on
7. from next Monday
8. until the end
9. by
10. on

5 Word study

1. d   2. f   3. b   4. g   5. a   6. i   7. j   8. c   9. h   10. e

Section B: Recruiting job candidates

Part 1: Job advertising

1 Warm-up

1.1 In the UK the most popular method is internal advertising.
1.2 In the UK the most popular is advertising in professional and trade journals.

2 Reading

Chart 3.4

Internal advertisement

Advantages: a. Maximum information to all employees, who might then act as recruiters
            b. Opportunity for all interested internal applicants to apply
            c. If an internal candidate is appointed there is a shorter induction period
            d. Speed
            e. Cost

Drawbacks: a. Possible discontent among unsuccessful candidates
            b. Limit to number of candidates
            c. 'Inbreeding'
            d. May be unlawful if indirect discrimination

Advertising in national press

Advantages: a. Advertisement reaches large numbers
            b. Some national newspapers are the accepted medium for search by those seeking particular posts

Drawbacks: a. Cost
            b. Much of the cost 'wasted' in reaching inappropriate people

Advertising in local press

Advantages: a. Recruitment ads more likely to be read by those seeking local employment
            b. Little 'wasted' circulation

Drawbacks: a. Local newspapers appear not to be used by professionals and technical people seeking vacancies

Advertising in technical press

Advantages: a. Reaches a specific population with minimum waste
            b. A minimum standard of applicant can be guaranteed

Drawbacks: a. Relatively infrequent publication may require advertising copy six weeks before appearance of advertisement
            b. Inappropriate where a non-specialist is needed, or where the specialist has a choice of professional publications.

---

3 Comprehension/interpretation

3.1 Hourly-paid, blue-collar.
3.2 The staff produced may only stay for a short time.
3.3 Because they can remain anonymous.
3.4 By allowing poor applicants to bypass the preliminary stages of the selection process.

---

4 *Language focus*

4.1   Connecting and sequencing ideas

    1   4   7   8   5   2   3   6

1. In other words/That means/That is to say
2. In particular
3. In fact
4. Alternatively
5. However
6. Overall

1. For example/instance
2. So/Therefore/Consequently
3. Similarly
4. Yet/However
5. Thus/So/Therefore
6. In addition/Furthermore
7. for instance/example

5 *Word study*

unhappy	**disappointed**	dissatisfied
demotivated		discontented

take on	**recruit**	hire
engage		appoint

expertise	**skill**	know-how
performance		competence

post	**job**	occupation
position		opening

Part 2: Selecting an advertising agency

1 Warm-up

1.1 Name and brief details of the employing organisation; job and duties; key points of the personnel specification, e.g. qualification, experience, age range; what to do next.

1.2 Possible reasons:
- The salary scales are well-known and inflexible.
- The employer does not want to publicise the salary for fear of dissatisfying holders of other posts.
- The employer does not know what to offer.

Listening tapescript

. . . as you can see from the benefits to our clients' businesses. So ads remain a good source of management recruitment – particularly for middle and senior management personnel.

Here at Lewis, Pemberton and Stott we use a four-point guide to ad design, called AIDA. And now I'd like to say a few words about the underlying principles of AIDA as a guide to effective ad design. I should say that it's not as theatrical as its name suggests! It is merely an acronym made up of four letters, and so, my short presentation will consist of four main points.

So, let's look first of all at the *A. A* stands for attention. In other words, first get the readers' attention. Well, if you look at this page from one of our leading dailies, you can easily see what I mean. This is an ad for one of our major pharmaceutical clients. If you compare it with some of the other ads on the page I'm sure you'll see what I mean. The closely printed text in this ad is lost, while ours, using this wide border effect, stands out. The same prominence can be achieved by using a lot of empty space – as in this ad for one of our international clients. For these reasons, key positions are best advertised in the display ads, where they don't get lost in the columns of classified ads, as you can see by looking at the effect of this page. So, that's the first step – getting the readers' attention.

Moving on to the next point. *I* stands for interest. Interest in the job itself. As you can see, interest may be created by the nature of the job itself, such as 'An International Challenge'. Sometimes, other aspects of the job, such as its location, can be used to create interest. Here a byline focusing on a factor of interest can be an effective strategy. So now we have attracted the reader's attention and whetted his or her appetite with an interesting selling point.

Next we come to *D* for desire. We need to create desire by amplifying on the interest factors plus the extras of the job. Here we can use aspects such as job satisfaction, career development, travel or similar attractions. But remember your target audience. The opportunity to work in a big city like London doesn't appeal to everyone, while the incentive of foreign travel can appear very attractive to certain professionals.

So, having whetted the appetite, we need to ensure that the appropriate action is taken. *A* stands for action. The ad should make it very clear what the interested party should do next – whether it's pick up the phone for an informal chat or send in a detailed cv.

Well, then, ladies and gentlemen, that is an overview of AIDA – our strategy in ensuring that you get the people you want. And now, if you have any questions, I'll be happy to answer them.

2 Listening

Chart 3.5

LEWIS, PEMBERTON AND STOTT

Patricia Eccleston – partner

Ads in management recruitment – good for middle and senior management.

A = Attention attracted by:	1.	Wide borders
	2.	A lot of empty space
I = Interest created by focusing on:	1.	The nature of the job itself
	2.	Aspects of the job
D = Desire created by amplifying:	1.	Interest factors
	2.	Extras of the job
A = Action, i.e. what to do next		

3 Comprehension/interpretation

3.1 Display ads and classified ads.
3.2 Location.
3.3 Job satisfaction, career development and travel.
3.4 Pick up the phone for an informal chat or send in a detailed cv.

4 Language focus

4.1 Presentations

The following sentences are *not* correct:

3. **By** that I mean interest in the job itself.
6. And now I'd like **to** say a few words about the underlying principles of AIDA as a guide to effective ad design.
7. So now we have attracted the readers' attention and whetted his or her appetite with an **interesting** selling point.
8. And now, if you have any **questions**, I'll be happy to answer them.
10. Moving on **to** the next point, *I* stands for interest.
11. I have divided my short presentation **into** four main points.
14. So, **let** me look first of all at the *A*.

The correct order is:

6   11   14   5   1   10   3   7   15   12   2   13   9   4   8

5 Word study

ad	advertisement
cv	curriculum vitae
e.g.	*exempli gratia* (for example)
i.e.	*id est* (that is)
no.	number
p.a.	per annum (per year)
c.	circa (about)
OTE	on-target earnings
t.o.	turnover
PC	personal computer
k	1,000 (used in salaries, e.g. 40k – sometimes K)
HRD	human resource(s) development
IT	information technology
DP	data processing

UNIT 4
Selection and interviewing

Section A: Selection methods

Part 1: Selection methods

1 Warm-up

1.1 Because of the expense of poor selection.

1.2 From a confident, ambitious person to a less outgoing one.

2 Reading

Chart 4.1

Application form	
Strengths:	a. Straightforward way of giving a standardised synopsis of applicant's history
	b. Helps applicants present their case within a predetermined structure
	c. Speeds sorting and shortlisting applicants
	d. Guides interviewers
Weaknesses:	a. Not many posts for which one can expect the applicants to complete lengthy forms
Telephone screening	
Strengths:	a. Speed
Weaknesses:	a. Decisions can be haphazard
	b. Difficult to set standards in advance
	c. Setting standards in advance may lead to too many or too few candidates
Testing	
Strengths:	a. More reliable than interviewing as predictor of performance
	b. Greater potential accuracy and objectivity
Weaknesses:	a. Dislike of tests' objectivity
	b. Difficulty of incorporating test evidence into other evidence collected
Group methods	
Strengths:	a. Provide examples of behaviour
Weaknesses:	a. Difficult to assess an individual's contribution
Work sampling	
Strengths:	a. Measure actual on-the-job performance
	b. The content of the work sample not as likely to be unfair to minorities
	c. Well-designed work samples almost always exhibit better validity than do tests designed to predict performance

3 Comprehension/interpretation

3.1 To get personal details as a nucleus of the personnel record.

3.2 Because they feel that they can improve their prospects by a good interview 'performance'.

3.3 Leaderless groups, command or executive exercises, and group problem solving.

3.4 To confirm the judgement of managers who have to make employment offers.

4 Language focus

4.1 Comparison of adjectives

1. more prevalent
2. larger
3. fewer
4. more
5. larger
6. biggest
7. more stringent/rigorous
8. more stringent/rigorous
9. most

4.2 Quantifiers

2. much sense
3. many motor ability skills
4. sometimes
5. most jobs
6. Only a few personality tests . . . all of them
7. a lot of uses, some valuable information
8. only a little job knowledge
9. A lot of organisations
10. Everybody . . . few

5 Word study

1. to act as
2. to apply oneself to
3. to ask for
4. to be based on
5. to deal with
6. to focus on
7. to incorporate into
8. to make use of
9. to point to
10. to provide someone with

6 *Transfer*

Suggested answers:

Predictor	Validity
Cognitive ability tests	Moderate
Physical ability tests	Moderate/high
Biographical information	Moderate
Interviews	Low
Work samples	High
Reference checks	Low
Academic performance	Low
Self-assessment	Moderate
Assessment centres	High

Part 2: Choosing selection methods

1 *Warm-up*

1.1 It provides information for decisions by both the employer and the potential employee.
1.2 Group selection methods and assessment centres.

Listening tapescript

PB: That brings us on to the next point – improving selection methods. Now, the background to this is that Sandra here has been assessing the costs of poor selection. And I would like to repeat what she said at the last meeting: that the time to screen out undesirables is before they have their foot in the door, not after. Now, I've put up here on the flipchart . . . the factors we need to take into account when choosing a selection method. Anyway, we are not looking for policy decisions here. It's simply an opportunity to exchange ideas at this stage. All right, so let's take a look at these points. Now, firstly I've put down acceptability and appropriateness, and by that I mean to the candidates involved. At one stage we put everyone joining the company through an intelligence test.

RD: Yes, and we found it fairly insulting in R&D that people with doctorates and other higher degrees should be subjected to IQ tests by the personnel department.

PB: Yes, and that's exactly why we phased it out at managerial level – it wasn't appropriate. And that underlines my point. If the selection method isn't acceptable or appropriate, we shouldn't use it.

SM: Actually, there was one point in favour of the IQ tests – they were easy to administer.

PB: Yes, I quite agree. I've got it up here on the chart. But the question of administrative ease is clearly subordinate to appropriateness.

SM: But surely not to accuracy? If we are talking about the cost of non-quality selection, we need to look at what method provides accurate selection. We mustn't forget our basic premise: that no one selection method is perfect. And therefore we need to look at that combination of methods which satisfies the greatest number of criteria.

PM: Yes, yes, I agree. But surely, if we find that methods A, B and C, for example, are accurate for selecting the right people for job Y, then we should implement that system – whether the candidates like it or not is an irrelevance.

RD: I think if we did that we would run the risk of making the people fit the system. Our job is to try and find a compromise . . . human solutions, if you like. So we have to be careful about imposing methods throughout the organisation. But if I may just add a couple of words about accuracy. The accuracy of selection increases in relation to the number of selection methods . . . sorry, the number of appropriate selection methods used. So if we extend our range of selection methods, we can expect to be more accurate.

SM: Fine, but I still think if we find a good combination for selecting certain staff grades, we should stick with it.

PB: Okay. Can I move on? Well, we've looked at acceptability and appropriateness, accuracy . . . and one of you mentioned administrative ease.

SM: Yes, I was saying the IQ tests were easy to administer. But I appreciate that we mustn't use selection procedures just because they are easy.

PB: Exactly. Here's an example that I'm sure you're all familiar with. Two candidates for a junior management post. Now, if we lived in an ideal world, you would run a panel interview with a panel of, say, four. Unfortunately your colleagues are not available, so you interview the candidates yourself. Not totally satisfactory, I think you'd agree.

RD: Yes, point taken, but sometimes we have to work under time pressures . . . we need to fill a position quickly . . . we can't afford the luxury of waiting till everyone is available.

PB: Again, I appreciate your point. In fact, I've put time factors on the chart as a key element. But I'd just like everyone to be aware that we need to balance all these criteria. In fact, we often resort to individual interviews because they are the easiest to set up. But if we had a better system of testing, we could reduce the time spent on interviewing.

RD: But not IQ tests!

SM: No, there are many test types.

RD: But who's going to develop them?

PB: Well, it's really for us to decide if we want to invest in a study, and then in the development of tests. The initial outlay would be high, but then they would be relatively cheap to administer. As Sandra has shown, cost is an important factor. If you look at the cost of assessment centres, you'll see that they involve a significant expense each time we run them, whereas tests would be cheap to run. The question is whether the improvement in selection decision-making would justify the cost.

2   Listening

In Chart 4.2:

1. Acceptability and appropriateness
2. Administrative ease
3. Accuracy
4. Time factors
5. Cost

3 Comprehension/interpretation

3.1 Before they have their foot in the door.

3.2 That people with doctorates and other higher degrees should be subjected to IQ tests by the personnel department.

3.3 That no one selection method is perfect.

3.4 Because they are the easiest to set up.

4 Language focus

4.1 Conditionals I and II

2. If the personnel manager was experienced, he or she may/might shortlist applicants alone.

3. If you wanted to appoint a new manager, you would usually use two or more selection methods.

4. If you want ease of administration, you should arrange individual interviews rather than panels.

5. If a position needed to be filled quickly, you might save time by using individual rather than group interviews.

6. If you want to increase the accuracy of your selection, you will have to use a larger number of appropriate selection methods.

7. If we decided to set up assessment centres, we would have to lay out quite a lot of money.

8. If we decide to continue with interviews, we can run them quite cheaply.

9. If we felt we wanted to change our procedure, we would all need to agree on the new methods.

10. If the procedure is changed, the costs will need to be calculated.

4.2 -ing and -ed clauses

2. Employers may ask for a factual reference after deciding/having decided to offer the job.

3. The knowledge of such a check being made is likely to encourage the candidate's truthfulness when applying for the job/making the job application.

4. The employer obtains a character reference before inviting the candidate for interview.

5. The information obtained (by the employer) is used in the decision-making process.

6. The validity of the character reference depends on the previous employer being a good judge of performance or not.

7. Candidates also influence the outcome by deciding whom to cite.

8. Candidates will clearly choose someone from whom they expect a favourable reference, perhaps even impressing on the referee the importance of positive remarks.

9. Consultants are increasingly involved in recruitment and selection, though rarely making the final decision themselves.

10. The consultants, being outsiders, are usually less able to judge how well a candidate will fit into the organisation.

5   Word study

Adjective	Noun
accurate	accuracy
appropriate	appropriateness/appropriacy
acceptable	acceptability
intelligent	intelligence
easy	ease
irrelevant	irrelevance
careful	care
relative	relation/relativity
available	availability
satisfactory	satisfaction
significant	significance
expensive	expense

Section B: Interviewing

Part 1: Interview structure and conduct

1   Warm-up

1.1   Usually because the interviewee feels, rightly or wrongly, that the interviewer is trying to find fault rather than being helpful.

2   Reading

Chart 4.3

Interview stage	Objectives	Activities
Beginning	1. Make the candidate feel at ease 2. Develop rapport 3. Set the scene	1. Greet candidate by name 2. Introduce self 3. Neutral chat 4. Sketch out plan of interview 5. Sketch out total employment decision process
Middle	1. Collect information 2. Give information 3. Maintain rapport	1. Asking questions within a structure (biographical or based on areas of information) 2. Listening 3. Observation 4. Answering questions
End	1. Close interview 2. Confirm future action	1. Summarise interview 2. Invite final questions 3. Indicate what happens next

3 Comprehension/interpretation

3.1 Wherever the candidate chooses a route that seems more promising.
3.2 Weather and traffic conditions.
3.3 Dress, appearance, voice, height and weight.
3.4 Listening and speaking.

4 Language focus

4.1 Verb constructions

2. She let him relax by talking about his journey to the interview.
3. First she asked him to talk about his education.
4. This safe ground enabled him to relax.
5. She permitted him to smoke.
6. She encouraged him to tell her about the responsibilities in his last job.
7. She helped him discuss his job by asking questions.
8. Finally she allowed him to ask her any questions he wanted.
9. I would prefer the working hours to be shorter.
10. She made him accept the job by offering a salary he couldn't refuse.

4.2 Verb + adjectives

1. comfortable
2. nervously
3. nervous
4. clearly
5. well
6. tense
7. lively . . . friendly
8. hardly
9. quickly
10. good

5 Word study

1. d   2. g   3. j   4. b   5. n   6. k   7. a   8. f   9. h   10. l   11. c   12. o
13. m   14. e   15. i

Part 2: Individual versus panel interviews

1 Warm-up

1.1 Greatest chance of establishing rapport; efficient deployment of time; usually most satisfactory for the candidate.
1.2 Shared judgement and decision; can perhaps lead to a quick decision.

Listening tapescript

DM: So, Sandra, here are the candidates whom we've shortlisted . . . there are six in all. The others have seen their CVs. Do you want to have a look?

SM: I'll have a look later.

DM: So, the purpose of this meeting is to decide what type of interview we're going to hold for the post of regional sales manager – individual or panel. From what Barry has said, there's now some urgency, and I'd like to try to set up the interviews for next week, if possible. Would you be available, Sandra?

SM: Available, . . . well, yes. I mean, I like to be involved in the selection process . . . but that doesn't mean I like running interviews. I'm available, if you feel you really need me. However, the appointee will need to work closely with all of you, and therefore you're the ones who know best what type of person you're looking for. So, that's my position.

DM: Well, as I think you all know I normally prefer individual interviews to panels. I feel I know the views of the department as well as its needs. However, I also know that there is a strong team spirit here – which I admire – and that some of you think that panels are more reliable. But I feel that I am in a pretty good position to make the final decision, especially as we're all fully agreed on the profile of the ideal candidate.

SM: So, what you're saying is that you'd like an individual interview.

DM: Exactly.

RM1: Well, I don't want this to turn into a debate about interviews. I know how Peter feels, but I would like him to realise that he's not the only one who has to work with the new regional sales manager. And I think it's important that we should make a joint decision.

SM: So, you'd like a panel interview?

RM1: Yes, I would. I mean, Peter, it's not that I don't trust your judgement. It's simply that this department has to work as a team, and the appointment of a new team member is important for all of us. I hope you can see it that way.

DM: Yes, I can. I've stated my preference, but I'm quite happy to accept the majority decision.

SM: Okay, thanks George. Patsy?

RM2: Well, I'm with Peter here. We've seen the CVs; we've graded them according to our preferences. As Peter is the person who'll have to deal most frequently and closely with the new person, I'd really prefer to leave the final decision to him.

SM: Yes, Patsy, but it's not just the question of who should make the decision. The point is rather who should sit in on the interview.

RM2: Yes, I've already said that I think Peter should interview the candidates and make his decision.

SM: Okay, Patsy, so you're for an individual interview, and you're happy to leave the inteviewing and the decision to Peter.

RM2: That's right.

SM: Barry?

RM3: I'd like to be in on the inteview. The strength of this department is based on the team spirit, and I think it would be a mistake to leave the decision to any one person – although, of course, Peter, I respect your views, and I don't want you to take this personally. It's just that I'd rather be safe than sorry – for all our sakes.

SM: Okay, thanks, Barry. So, the situation seems to be two in favour of an individual interview and two for a panel. Peter, do you want to say something?

DM: Yes. Okay, to resolve the problem, I'll change my position. I don't want this to be an issue. My concern is to find the best person, that's all.

SM: Okay, fine, Peter. Is that okay with you, Patsy?

RM3: Yes, that's okay with me.

SM: Good. So now that we've got agreement about the type of interview, the next question is who will sit on the panel. Four is not the best size for a panel.

RM3: Well, let me say that I'm quite happy not to sit on the panel. If that's okay with the others.

DM: Yes.

RM1: Okay.

RM2: Fine.

SM: Good, that's it then. Peter.

DM: So, I'll try and set up the inteviews for next Wednesday. I hope that's still okay for everybody.

RM1: Yes.

RM2: Fine.

RM1: But will you confirm it please, Peter?

DM: Yes, of course. I'll let you know as soon as Margaret has spoken to the candidates. Well, Sandra, thanks for your time.

SM: Not at all.

2 Listening

Chart 4.4

| | Preference | | Interviewer |
	Individual	Panel	
Sandra	—	—	
Peter	✓		✓
George		✓	✓
Patsy	✓		
Barry		✓	✓

3 Comprehension/interpretation

3.1 Six.

3.2 Because the appointee will need to work closely with the sales team, and they are the ones who know best what type of person they are looking for.

3.3 I'm quite happy to accept the majority decision.

3.4 The following Wednesday.

4   Language focus

4.1   Likes and preferences

1. B: No thanks, you know I *don't like running* inteviews – I just don't enjoy it.
2. This is Mary Bell. Right, Mrs Bell, *would you like to sit down*?
3. A: Would you like to discuss the interview now or *would you rather discuss* it later?
   B: If possible, I *would prefer to evaluate* each candidate immediately after their interview.

1. a
2. b
3. b
4. a
5. c
6. a

4.2   The future with **going to** and **will**

2. A: So, what are you planning to do first?
   B: Well, first we are going to contact a number of recruitment agencies.
3. It is likely that three or four agencies will be able to help.
4. We've now chosen one agency. I've contacted them to give them the brief. So, I'll contact you as soon as I've heard from them.
5. A: In fact, I'm a little worried about their fees.
   B: So, what are you going to do?
   A: First I'm going to discuss the fees with the MD
6. When are you going to see the MD?
7. I've arranged a meeting for this afternoon. I'm pretty sure he will make a quick decision.
8. A: So when can you call me?
   B: I'll call you as soon as I've spoken to him.
9. If we use the same agency as last time, I know it will be expensive.
10. In that case, leave it with me. I'll look into other possibilities, but I'm not too hopeful.

5   Word study

1. to deal with the new person
2. to make a decision
3. to have a look
4. to sit on the panel
5. to set up the interview
6. to look for a person
7. to agree on the profile
8. to turn into a debate
9. to be in on the interview
10. to run an interview

UNIT 5
Training and development

Section A: Training

Part 1: Determining training needs

1 *Warm-up*

1.1 Difficulty of identifying and demonstrating results; the lack of external controls; dis-interest in training among personnel and other managers.

2 *Reading*

Step 1: Performance appraisal
Step 2: Cost/value analysis
Step 3: Distinguish between 'can't do' and 'won't do' problems
Step 4: Set standards
Step 5: Eliminate obstacles in the system
Step 6: Practice
Step 7: Training
Step 8: Change the job
Step 9: Transfer or terminate
Step 10: Reward or punishment

In Chart 5.1:

a. Cost/value analysis
b. Distinguish between 'can't do' and 'won't do' problems
c. Set standards
d. Motivate employee
e. Eliminate obstacles in the system
f. Practice
g. Training
h. Change the job
i. Transfer or eliminate

3 *Comprehension/interpretation*

3.1 The difference between the person's current performance and what you would like it to be.
3.2 Distinguishing between 'can't do' and 'won't do' problems.
3.3 Transfer or terminate.
3.4 Motivation.

4 Language focus

4.1 Verb + preposition

1. involved in
2. hope for
3. discuss
4. looking for
5. listen to
6. distinguish between
7. expected of/from
8. speak to/with (Am.E.)
9. stopping them (from)
10. reach
11. praised for
12. look again at
13. Ask your employees
14. help with

4.2 Verb . . . *ing*

3. There are other methods of/for rectifying deficiencies.
4. You should consider other possibilities, such as changing the machinery.
5. You should start by identifying the discrepancy between present performance and target performance.
6. It is worth first determining what the person's present performance is.
7. But perhaps the cost of solving the problem is out of proportion to the benefits.
8. Sometimes not solving a problem is cheaper than investing in a training programme.
9. You can distinguish between different types of deficiency problem by asking three sets of questions.
10. Perhaps the worker has trouble understanding what is expected.
11. While speaking with a worker, you may find out that he or she doesn't know the extent of the deficiencies.
12. They might suggest taking some simple steps to improve performance.
13. Sometimes workers waste time having to wait for materials at their work stations.
14. So you can often look forward to remedying deficiencies without major expenditure.

5 Word study

1. c   2. e   3. g   4. i   5. f   6. a   7. l   8. j   9. d   10. h   11. b   12. k

Part 2: Setting up an induction programme

1 Warm-up

1.1 Tense and nervous.

1.2 To minimise tension and anxiety by introducing the new employee and the organisation to each other.

Listening tapescript

SM: Right, that was very good, George. So the main points for the first day of employment were:

1. Introduction to fellow workers
2. Information about:

- the toilets and washrooms
- the coffee machine, and
- lunch

Was there anything else?

S1: Yes, the notice-board.

SM: Right, the notice-board. . . . Fine, so that was the first section. Let's look at the second part about rules and policies. Now, I realise that the actual information in your cases will be slightly different, but what I'd like to do now is listen to some little presentations and then we can build up our points for the checklist.

Now Mary, you said you'd got a little talk that you give to your new secretaries.

S2: Yes, this is a brief introduction for secretaries working in admin.

SM: Right, Mary.

S2: Right. Good morning, I'd like to welcome you to Codix. Now you all know which sections you are going to, but before you meet your section heads, I'd like to tell you something about the rules and policies at Codix. Why do we need rules? Well, it's simply that they help us all to know what we can do, what we must do and what we shouldn't do – and in the long run to make this a happy place to work.

So, first of all, hours. We have a flexitime system here. That means you can choose what time you are going to start and finish. However, you must all be here for core time from 10 till 3. You should all work for a minimum of 37 hours a week, and normally you shouldn't put in more than 41 hours. If you look at your job descriptions you'll see that the average is 38.5 hours per week. This means you can put in and claim for an extra 2.5 hours per week. However, at the end of any month you mustn't have more than 10 hours' overtime, because that's the maximum that can be claimed. Is that clear?

Okay, I've mentioned pay for overtime. Let's look at pay generally. You've each got the details of your basic pay rates and your overtime pay rates. Now you will all receive your pay on the last Friday of the month. This won't be a full month, but you'll all receive some pay. It'll be paid directly into your bank or building society accounts. So, if you want to be paid this month, you must give your account details to your section heads. If anybody has any questions about deductions, we can look at those after you've received your first pay slip. Right, are there any questions about pay? Of course, there's always someone who hasn't got any money, or hasn't got an account. Anyway . . .

Good. So, now let's look at holidays. You all have eighteen days' holiday a year. Ten of these eighteen days must be taken during July when we are closed. The other eight days may be taken in either one or two instalments, for example five days and three days or six days and two days. But you can't have eight separate single days off or four two-day periods off. If you have any questions about holidays. I can answer them later.

Next is the probationary period. The probationary period here is one month. I hope that you will all complete it successfully and won't have any problems with your work. But if you do, please do go and talk to your section heads or come and have a chat with me.

On to absences and sickness. If you fall ill, please inform your section head as soon as you possibly can – ideally first thing in the morning. That's very important because it's your section head who will need to arrange cover if you are likely to be away for a longer period. And if we don't have any cover, it's hard for the others who have to take over your work. Now under the present regulations a sick note is not required during the first seven days of absence. If, however, you should be absent for longer, then you should arrange to see your doctor and ask for a sick note. If you don't, we can't pay you. Okay?

Right, the next section is about the organisation of the department. I'm not going to do that bit now, if you don't mind. I usually take the new secretaries through from organisation to divisions to departments to sections. Then finally, BR – basic rules. This part is a pep talk about punctuality, using the phone and general behaviour. Then I thank them for their attention and hand over to the section heads.

SM: Well, Mary, thank you very much. That's really good. Now let's have a look at the main areas that Mary covered.

2 Listening

Chart 5.2

ITEMS TO BE DISCUSSED BY DEPARTMENT HEAD OR SUPERVISOR
WITH NEW EMPLOYEE

First day of employment
1. Introduction to fellow workers
2. Information on:
   - The toilets and washrooms
   - The coffee machine
   - Lunch
   - The notice-board

Roles and policies
1. Hours:
   - Starting time
   - Finishing time
   - Hours per week
   - Overtime
2. Pay:
   - When paid
   - Where paid
   - How paid
3. Holidays
4. Probationary period
5. Absences:
   - Who to inform
   - When to inform
   - Sick notes
6. Organisation of department
7. Basic rules:
   - Punctuality
   - Using the phone
   - General behaviour

3 Comprehension/interpretation

3.1 Flexitime; core time.
3.2 Ten hours.
3.3 Directly into their bank or building society accounts.
3.4 Seven days.

4 Language focus

4.1 Modals of ability, possibility and necessity

2. With the flexitime system you must all be here from 10 till 3.
3. You mustn't put in more than 41 hours per week.
4. With the flexitime system you can claim for an extra 2½ hours per week.
5. In the past, according to company regulations you could claim 8 hours' overtime pay per month.
6. In the past, according to company regulations you also had to get authorisation for overtime.
7. Now according to company regulations you needn't get authorisation for overtime.
8. Under no circumstances can we provide an advance on salary.
9. According to company regulations we can't/mustn't take all our holiday entitlement in summer.
10. If you fall ill, you needn't supply a sick note during the first seven days of absence.

4.2 Some, any and related words

1. First I'd like to give you some information about the toilets and washrooms.
2. If somebody/someone/anybody/anyone wants to put something/anything up on the notice board, please feel free.
3. This is a short presentation that I sometimes give to the new secretaries.
4. That sounds fine. Do you ever/sometimes talk about the social side?
5. That question seems somewhat complex. Do you mind if I take it at the end of this session?
6. Right. Are there any/some more questions?
7. Well, have you seen my notes? I can't find them anywhere.
8. First of all I'd like to tell you all something about the rules and regulations here.
9. You may be wondering why we need rules at all.
10. You need to decide some time before next Monday if you want to work the early shift or the late shift.
11. I don't think I've got anything else to say.
12. If there is anything at all you want to ask, now is the time.

5 Word study

sickness	overtime	organisation	chat
absence	flexitime	department	presentation
illness	core time	section	pep talk
sick note	starting time	division	introduction

Section B: Development

Part 1: On-the-job training methods

1 Warm-up

1.1 It is concerned with developing the whole person; it emphasises the contribution of formal and informal work experiences; it places greater responsibility on managers to develop themselves; it is concerned with both present jobs and future jobs.

1.2 You develop an organisation by developing the managers and vice versa.

2 Reading

Chart 5.3

Training approach	Suitable for	Objectives
1. Job rotation	Management trainees	1. Helps broaden the person's experience 2. Helps the person discover the jobs he or she prefers
2. Coaching/ understudy	Junior management	1. Gives the trainee a chance to perform an increasing range of management tasks and gradually learn the job. 2. Helps ensure that the employer will have trained managers to assume key positions
3. Junior boards	Young middle management	1. Give promising young middle managers experience in analysing overall company problems. 2. Give trainees top-level analysis and policy-making experience
4. Action learning	Middle management	1. Gives trainees real experience with actual problems 2. Develops skills like problem analysis and planning
5. Mentoring	Junior and middle management	1. Enhances career development 2. Enhances a sense of competence, clarity of identity and effectiveness in the managerial role

3 Comprehension/interpretation

3.1 General line managers.

3.2 Discussion, exhortation, encouragement and understanding.

3.3 The employer loses the full-time services of a competent managers, while the trainee often finds it hard to return to his or her old position.

3.4 Information peers, collegial peers, special peers.

4   Language focus

4.1   Relative clauses

1. On-the-job training, which includes job rotation, coaching, junior boards, and under-study assignments, is one of the most popular development methods.
2. Job trainees spend time in each department, where they broaden their experience.
3. The trainee becomes involved in the business whose activities he or she learns more about.
4. Job rotation has several advantages, the most important of which is that it provides a well-rounded training experience for each person.
5. The coaching/understudy approach is particularly useful for junior-management train-ees, who will work directly under the person whom/that/∅/they will replace.
6. This approach helps ensure that the employer will have trained managers in the future, when the posts will need to be filled.
7. 'Junior' board of directors, the members of which come from various departments, are composed of promising young middle managers.
8. The protégés who are chosen must be good performers and come from the right social background.
9. Peer relationships, which can provide a number of benefits for the development of both individuals, are very common.

4.2   Comparing and contrasting ideas

2. Non-managers are likely to receive technical training for their present job, while managers are likely to receive assistance in developing skills for future jobs.
3. It is easy to offer training programmes. But/Yet/However, it is more difficult to change behaviour.
4. Despite an improvement in/of knowledge, training programmes do not necessarily improve effectiveness.
5. Off-the-job training takes place outside the actual workplace; in contrast on-the-job training takes place in it.
6. Despite the focus on workplace skills, on-the-job training is also likely to include classroom instruction.
7. Role-playing can be an enjoyable and inexpensive way to develop many new skills. However/Yet, some trainees feel that it is childish.
8. Although on-the-job experience is by far the most popular form of management development, the preferred techniques differ according to organisational level.

5   Word study

1. job rotation
2. staff expert
3. career development
4. trainee manager or management trainee
5. development method
6. company problems
7. executive compensation
8. action learning
9. problem analysis
10. information peers

Part 2: Reviewing the development needs

1 Warm-up

1.1 These include counselling, training, motivating, appraising and writing.

1.2 Because they give trainees realistic experience in identifying and analysing complex problems in an environment where their progress can be guided by a trained leader.

Listening tapescript

S1: John Graham's office.

DO: Hello, this is Dianne O'Connor from the training department here. Could I speak to John Graham please?

S1: I'm sorry, John's gone down to our Hoverton plant. He was called down urgently this morning to sort out a problem.

DO: When will he be back?

S1: I don't think he'll be back before Monday.

DO: Okay, thank you.

S1: Bye.

DO: Bye. Right, now where did I put the Hoverton plant number? Right. 0745 578453.

S2: Codix, can I help you?

DO: Yes, this is Dianne O'Connor from head office here. I'm trying to get through to John Graham, one of our operations supervisors. Apparently he's down there with you. Can you find him for me, please?

S2: I'll try. Hold the line, please . . . You're through now.

S3: Operations.

DO: Hello, this is Dianne O'Connor from head office here. Is John Graham with you?

S3: Yes, just a moment please, Mrs O'Connor.

JG: Hello, John Graham speaking.

DO: Hello, John, this is Dianne O'Connor. I'm just phoning to . . .

JG: Yes, I know exactly why you're calling. I've forgotten to send that questionnaire back to you. It's here in my case. You see, I got called down here urgently . . . I was going to ring you later.

DO: That's okay. It's just that I'm seeing Philip Bradshaw later today, so I'd like to have all the responses.

JG: Right, just hang on . . . Okay, I've got it in front of me now. Would you like me to read what I've put down?

DO: Oh, yes please.

JG: Right. For the first one on motivating others, I've got high priority.

DO: Right.

JG: The next one on evaluation and appraisal I've got as a medium priority.

DO: Uh huh, right.

JG: Then the next two – that's leadership and oral communication – I've got as high priority.

DO: Right.

JG: Then for developing and training subordinates I've got . . .

DO: Sorry, John, you've missed one out.

JG: So I have. So, understanding human behaviour – low priority. At the moment, it's the machines I wish I could understand.

DO: Is it a serious problem?

JG: One of the process control machines is down, and the chocolate mixture is like rock. Anyway, where were we?

DO: Developing and training.

JG: Yes, I've put that one and the next as medium priority.

DO: Right.

JG: Then written communication – low priority.

DO: And the last one?

JG: Yes, high priority for that.

DO: Right, John, many thanks.

JG: Not at all. Sorry for causing the inconvenience.

DO: Oh, that's okay. I hope you sort out your problem.

JG: Our problem, Dianne.

DO: Okay, Bye.

JG: Bye.

DO: Right, now all I have to do is to collate all these responses.

2 Listening

Chart 5.4

TO: Junior managers
FROM: Dianne O'Connor, training and development manager

Please indicate your needs by ticking the appropriate box and return to me not later than Wednesday, 22 April.
Name: John Graham

Position: Operations supervisor

Development needs	**Priority**		
	High	Medium	Low
1. Motivating others	✓		
2. Evaluation and appraisal		✓	
3. Leadership	✓		
4. Oral communication	✓		
5. Understanding human behaviour			✓
6. Developing and training subordinates		✓	
7. Setting objectives and priorities		✓	
8. Written communication			✓
9. Selecting employees	✓		

3 Comprehension/interpretation

3.1 To sort out a problem.

3.2 Because she's seeing Philip Bradshaw, the personnel director, later that day.

3.3 One of the process control machines has gone down, and the chocolate mixture is like rock.

3.4 To collate all the responses.

4 Language focus

4.1 Telephoning

CONVERSATION 1

A: Ann Gordon. (1)
B: Hello, this is Alan Clark from the training department here. Could I speak to John Graham please? (2)
A: I'm sorry, John's in a meeting at the moment. (3)
B: Oh, I see. (4)
A: D'you know when he'll be back in the office? (5)
B: No, I'm afraid not. Can I take a message? (6)
A: Yes, please. Could you ask him to phone me when he gets back? (7)
B: Yes, certainly. (8)
A: Right, thanks. (9)
B: By the way, could you give me your extension? (10)
A: Yes, it's 1076. (11)
B: Right. Bye. (12)
A: Bye. (13)

CONVERSATION 2

B: Alan Clark. (1)
A: Hello, Alan. John Graham here. (2)
B: Oh, hello John. How are you? (3)
A: Fine thanks. Alan, I'm just returning your call. (4)
B: Yes, thanks. (5)
A: So, what can I do for you? (6)
B: Well, it's about the training course. (7)
A: You mean the French one? (8)
B: Yes, that's right. (9)
A: The training centre need to know when you can attend. (10)
B: Let me see. I've put down week 43. (11)
A: Fine. I'll give them the information. (12)
B: Do I need to contact them myself? (13)
A: No, they'll be in touch with you. (14)
B: Right, John, that's all I wanted to know. (15)
A: Bye for now. (16)
B: Bye. (17)

5 Word study

1. c   2. e   3. g   4. b   5. h   6. a   7. f   8. d

UNIT 6

Compensation, incentives and benefits

Section A: Pay

Part 1: What the employee expects from the payment contract

1 Warm-up

1.1 Compensation means payment for loss or injury; reward means special payment for a special act.

1.2 Wages tend to be paid weeky, salaries monthly. Wages tend to be paid in cash; salaries by cheque or bank transfer. Salaried employees are likely to see themselves as doing a piece of management's job; wage earners see themselves as doing the work that management would never do.

2 Reading

First objective: Purchasing power
Second objective: 'Felt fair'
Third objective: Rights
Fourth objective: Relativities
Fifth objective: Composition

Chart 6.1

	Basic rate	Overtime	Incentives	Benefits
Younger workers	✓	✓	✗	✗
Older workers	✓	O	O	✓
The low-paid	✓	✓	O	✗
Married women	✓	✗	O	O
Long-term employees	O	O	✓	O
White-collar employees	O	O	O	✓

3 Comprehension/interpretation

3.1   Inflation and rising expectations.
3.2   By looking for another job, carelessness, disgruntlement, lateness, and absence.
3.3   'To each according to his needs' or 'a fair day's pay'.
3.4   First is the definition of pay. Second is the method of measuring changes; absolute amount of money or percentage. Third is the choice of pay dates.

4 Language focus

4.1   Genitive forms

2. the beginning of last week
3. the chairman's resignation
4. the departments' debts/the debts of the departments
5. the improvement of our trading position
6. the regions' economic prospects
7. the agenda of today's meeting
8. the targets of the division/the division's targets
9. the effect of the late delivery
10. the decision of the banks/the banks' decision

4.2   Each, every and all

1. *Wrong*: each piece of equipment/all the equipment
2. *Wrong*: each of the contracts
3. *Wrong*: all the jobs
4. *Right*
5. *Wrong*: Everyone

1. everything
2. each/all
3. every
4. everywhere
5. every/each

5 Word study

Verbs	Nouns
pay	payment
receive	recipient/reception
satisfy	satisfaction
earn	earnings
consider	consideration
adjust	adjustment
reduce	reduction
expect	expectation
evaluate	evaluation
withdraw	withdrawal
exist	existence
entitle	entitlement
divide	division
argue	argument
enjoy	enjoyment
compare	comparison/comparator
vary	variation
choose	choice
arrange	arrangement
differ	difference

Part 2: What the employer expects from the payment contract

1 Warm-up

1.1 Examples include: overtime rates, bonuses, incentive payments, sick pay, accommodation allowance, and company car.

1.2 In the UK the situation is typically as follows:

Manual unskilled	– waged
Semi-skilled	– waged
Clerical/secretarial	– salaried
Supervisory	– salaried

Listening tapescript

PB: Good evening, everybody. I'd like to welcome you all to this evening's presentation on 'The contract for payment – the employer's objectives'. As always, I am pleased to see the that so many of you have managed to come. I'm also delighted to welcome our speaker this evening. Frank Field is a member of PAB – the Payment Advisory Board – as well as running a consultancy advising management in the field of industrial relations. He is therefore well qualified to lead this evening's session. I have discussed the programme outline with Frank, and we have agreed that he will speak for about one hour. That'll take us up to 9 o'clock, when we will have a half-hour break. The second session will be an opportunity for questions from the audience and discussion for about one hour. That means we will end at 10.30 or thereabouts. I hope that covers the basic administration. And so now, Frank, over to you.

FF: Well, thank you very much, Philip. At this stage I normally give a little introduction of myself, but as Philip has done such a grand job, I'd like to start off by reminding you of the employer's five objectives for the contract of employment. After that I'd like to look at each of these in more detail, and finally I'd like to consider the implications of these in practice.

So let's now look at these five objectives. Firstly, there is prestige for the organisation. There is a comfortable and understandable conviction that it is 'a good thing' to be a good payer. The basis is partly a matter of simple pride at doing better than the others, and partly a feeling that if you are a good, or even the best, payer in the area then this policy eliminates a variable from the contractual relationship. An example of what I mean is the chief executive who said: 'I want to find out the highest rates of pay, job-for-job, within a fifty mile radius of this office. Then I will make sure that I raise the rates for all my boys by 20 per cent over that. Then I know where I am because I've taken money out of the equation. If they want to leave, they can't hide the real reason by saying it's because of the money; and if I do have to fill a job I know that we won't lose a good guy because the money isn't right.'

Of course, whether high pay rates succeed in getting an organisation the reputation of being a good employer is difficult to say. What seems much more likely, however, is that the low-paying organisation will have the reputation of being a poor employer.

So that was prestige. Next comes competition. This is a more rational approach to the question of rates. It's based on paying what is sufficiently competitive to attract and keep the right number of staff. Not just staff, but suitably qualified and experienced employees. So, the right type of staff for the organisation. So there's clearly a distinction between competition-thinking and prestige-thinking. The former aims to get a good fit on one of the dimensions of the employment contract, i.e. pay, rather than simply overwhelm it. Of course, it raises all kinds of questions, such as, 'How selective do we need to be for this range of jobs?' and 'How can we avoid overpaying people?' But I'll come back to these questions and others later.

Thirdly we have control: control of payment operations. There may be many ways of organising the pay packet that will facilitate control of operations and potentially reduce payment costs. Now, traditionally, there have been two methods. The conventional approach to this question for many years has been the use of piecework or similar incentives. But in recent times this has become difficult due to the unwillingness of most employees to see their pay fluctuate wildly. Good pay packets when times were good; poor pay packets when times were bad; the employer had control. The second approach was, in theory at least, overtime. The employer could use this to control output through making available or withholding additional payment. In practice, it's the employees who have come to use overtime as a control method more extensively than the employers. And, gradually, other ways in which the employer could control wage costs are being eliminated or made more difficult by legislation. As we all know, redundancy, short-term lay-offs and dismissals are all now more expensive; the pool of women as a reservoir of in-expensive, temporary labour has decreased substantially; and part-time employees now have to be nationally insured on exactly the same basis as full-time employees.

So the area of control is one we need to address through new methods. Again, I'll come back to this point later.

On to the fourth objective – motivation and productivity. There is a widespread conviction about the motivational effect of payments. In my opinion this is based on over-simplistic assumptions about amounts and methods of payment, such as if payments rise, so will motivation and productivity. So some features of payment and its influences are worth mentioning here.

Incentive payment schemes have been used extensively in industry as the basis for paying manual workers. These schemes have a built-in bias towards volume rather than quality of output. The following two examples – somewhat extreme – will show the weakness of this approach. Let's imagine someone engaged in the manufacture of diamond-tipped drilling bits. This employee would serve his employer badly if payment were linked to output. If it were possible to devise a payment method that contained an incentive linked to high quality of workmanship or on low scrap value, then that system might be more effective. Let's take schoolteachers as our second example. If they were paid a 'quantity bonus', it would presumably be based either on the number of children in the class or on some other measurable factor such as the number of examination classes. The first would encourage teachers to take classes as large as possible – with, probably, adverse effects on the quality of teaching. The second might increase the proportion of children succeeding in exams, but would isolate those who could not produce impressive exam results. Again a point to return to.

Finally we have cost. Just as employees are interested in purchasing power – the absolute value of their earnings – so employers are interested in cost – the absolute cost of payment – and, of course, its bearing on the profitability of the organisation. The importance of this cost varies between industries: in petroleum refining employment costs are minimal; in teaching or nursing they are substantial. So, the employer's interest in this objective obviously increases with the significance of employment costs in the organisation – not only in the short term but also in the long term. Not only do employees expect their incomes to be maintained and to carry on rising – rather than fluctuating with company profitability – but they also have expectations set up by pay rises. A settlement of x per cent this year will set up an expectation of at least x per cent next year. And so the cycle continues.

Anyway, those are the five objectives for the employer. Are there any questions at this . . .

2 Listening

Chart 6.2

Objectives	Basis
1. Prestige	1. Pride
	2. Elimination of a variable from the contractual relationship
2. Competition	1. Paying what is sufficiently competitive to attract and keep:
	• the right number of staff
	• the right type of staff
3. Control	1. Incentives, e.g. piecework
	2. Overtime
4. Motivation and productivity	1. Incentive payments
5. Cost	1. The significance of employment costs in the organisation

3 Comprehension/interpretation

3.1 Poor employers.

3.2 Redundancy, short-term lay-offs and dismissals; women as a reservoir of inexpensive, temporary labour; and part-time employees.

3.3 They have a built-in bias towards volume rather quality of output.

3.4 That it will be maintained; that it will continue to rise; that future settlements will be at least as high as the present settlement.

4 Language focus

4.1 Cause and effect

2. We pay well because of the prestige that it gives us.

3. We feel proud to be good payers because/since we know that we are doing something better than others.

4. Workers can't say low pay causes them to leave.

5. Our competitors pay poorly. Therefore they can't attract the quality of worker that we can.

6. We base our payment on piecework because of its simplicity to administer.

7. Fluctuations in pay packets can result from piecework.

8. Employees use overtime more extensively than the employers. So they effectively control it.

9. The decrease of the pool of women as a reservoir of inexpensive, temporary labour has led to the employers' loss of this cheap source of labour.

10. It is simplistic to assume that worker motivation and productivity will rise because payments are increased.

4.2 Increase and decrease

2. If we put up our rates, then we have taken money out of the equation.

3. If there is a decrease in a company's rates, then it will certainly get the reputation of being a poor employer.

4. If we want to recruit suitably qualified staff, we mustn't drop our rates any further.

5. We mustn't cut control of payment operations.

6. In fact we must have/make a reduction of payment costs.

7. Piecework can cause pay to increase and decrease dramatically.

8. There have been sharp rises/has been a sharp rise in the costs of redundancy, short-term lay-offs and dismissals.

9. It is important in our industry that we keep employment costs stable.

10. Employees have expectations that their pay will rise.

5 Word study

1. N	g	9. V	b
2. V	j	10. N	k
3. V	d	11. V	a
4. Adv	p	12. Adv	f
5. N	i	13. Adv	e
6. Adj	h	14. Adj	m
7. N	l	15. Adj	n
8. Adj	c	16. Adv	o

Section B: Incentives and benefits

Part 1: Developing effective incentive plans

1 Warm-up

1.1 Because they believe that money motivates people to be more productive.
1.2 The widespread use of incentives is due to three things: tradition, the unsupervised nature of most sales work, and the assumption that incentives are needed to motivate salespeople. The main reason for using straight salaries is where your salespeople are primarily involved in finding new clients or servicing existing accounts.

2 Reading

1. Ensure that effort and rewards are directly related
2. The reward must be valuable to the employees
3. Study methods and procedures carefully
4. The plan must be understandable and easily calculable by the employees
5. Set effective standards
6. Guarantee your standards
7. Guarantee an hourly base rate

3 Comprehension/interpretation

3.1 The person must believe that effort on his or her part will lead to reward, and he or she must want that reward.
3.2 They will see that the production levels of group members are held down.
3.3 Very careful observation and measurement by an industrial engineer or other methods expert.
3.4 Because once standards have been set, they represent a contract between the employer and the employees. By changing the standards, the employer is viewed as breaking his side of the contract.

4 Language focus

4.1 Advising and suggesting

2. I (would) recommend you to look at the area of human motivation.
   I (would) recommend (that) you look at the area of human motivation.
3. They suggested that we (should) set attainable standards.
4. Why don't we make the incentive plans simpler?
5. I think you should communicate the plan to the employees in an understandable way.
6. Let's look at the reasons why incentive plans fail.
7. How about focusing on some of the causes of failure?
8. It's advisable to prepare some specific guidelines for developing effective incentive plans.
9. (I suggest that) you ought to reward employees in direct proportion to their increased productivity.
10. Why don't you provide better tools, equipment and training?
11. The methods expert suggested that he (should) provide an attractive reward.
12. Let's build our incentive plans on fair performance standards.

4.2   Degree with **very** and **too**

1. too	6. very
2. very	7. too/very
3. Very	8. very
4. too/very	9. very/too
5. very	10. very

5   *Word study*

1. e   2. d   3. f   4. h   5. a   6. c   7. j   8. i   9. b   10. g

Part 2: Reducing management fringe benefits

1   *Warm-up*

1.1   Incentives are usually paid to specific employees whose work is above standard; benefits are available to all employees based on their membership of the organisation.

1.2   In the UK perks include:

> company car
> free private medical insurance
> non-contributory pension scheme
> personal loan facility at reduced rate of interest
> subsidised house mortgage
> profits-related bonus scheme

Listening tapescript

PB: Well, we still have time for some more questions. Would anybody else like to ask a question? Yes, Peter, your question, please.

Q2:   First of all I'd like to say that I agree with you, John, on the cost factor of fringe benefits. So, I'd like to ask you what you suggest that we do about them or with them?

JG: Well, quite frankly, I would recommend that every company scrap them or, if they can't do that, then at least give control of them to the personnel department.

Q2:   Why exactly do you say that?

JG: Well, I think we'd all agree that if these fringe benefits are to play any significant role in our field of activities – in personnel – then two general points flow logically from this. Firstly they must be incorporated – firmly incorproated – within payment policy; and secondly they must be administered by the personnel department.

Q2:   So, you'd advise us to take over control of the fringe benefit schemes in our companies.

JG: Yes, I'd certainly advise you to take control of them – or at least to try. My pessimism is based on my experience that the majority of these schemes are outside personnel's control. But my main concern about them is that there seems little sense of purpose about why they are provided and what they are to achieve. I mean membership of the local health club, for example. I know we live in an age where executive health is an important consideration. But could you tell me why it's offered? It's offered because it's a good bargain – the employer can probably get it half price – so it seems like too good an opportunity to miss. Many benefits are provided simply because it's the accepted practice.

Q2: It's easy for you to advise us to take over control – but how? What should we be doing?

JG: Well, that's a good question. The way forward, in my opinion, is to start by asking yourselves and your company a series of questions about the rationale of fringe benefits. First of all, identify them. What are the benefits? Make a list and find out who gets what. Then ask yourself, 'What is each of these benefits for?' And then, 'Does it achieve its purpose?', 'Does the organisation benefit?' And if your answer is still yes, then ask yourself, 'Is that purpose, that benefit to the organisation worth achieving?' Those are higher-level general questions to justify the existence of fringe benefits.

Q2: You mentioned before the problem of control and said that these benefits should be administered by the personnel department. Could you say a bit more about that, please?

JG: Yes, certainly. I said that fringe benefits should be firmly incorporated within payment policy and administered by the personnel department. So the next question to ask is, 'Who administers the various schemes?' and 'Is that the appropriate person or department?' In my experience fringe benefit schemes have grown up without any overall control, and each part of the scheme is jealously guarded by one person. So, in effect, there is no overall control and thus no way of ensuring that it is run for the benefit of the organisation. So, with those questions we've moved on to look at the practicalities of administration. And then you've got to look at cost. Here you need to ask, 'How much does each feature cost?', 'How much trouble does it cause?' It's not simply the cost of providing the feature, it's also the administrative costs involved in setting up and maintaining these different schemes which are also significant. So those, then, are questions about costs. And then, when you've collected all your data, you can start to see whether the benefits to the organisation outweigh the drawbacks. My feeling is that unless fringe benefits are positively managed, they can become an expensive and ineffective element in the employment relationship. Well, I hope that answers your question about my views on perks.

PB: Yes, thanks very much John, I think that we have time for one last question. Right, the lady in the red sweater.

Q3: Yes, I just wanted to comment on some of the points . . .

2 Listening

Chart 6.3

1. General points
   - They must be firmly incorporated within payment policy
   - They must be administered by the personnel department

2. Recommended action
   - Companies to scrap fringe benefits
   - Personnel department to take control

3. General questions to justify their existence
   - What is each of these benefits for?
   - Does it achieve its purpose
   - Does the organisation benefit?
   - Is that purpose/benefit to the organisation worth achieving?

4. Administration questions
   - Who administers the various schemes?
   - Is that the appropriate person or department?

5. Cost questions
   - How much does each feature cost?
   - How much trouble does it cause?

3 Comprehension/interpretation

3.1 Because in his experience the majority of these schemes are outside personnel's control.
3.2 Simply because it's the accepted practice.
3.3 Because there is no overall control.
3.4 Fringe benefits can become an expensive and ineffective element in the employment relationship.

4 Language focus

4.1 Questions and requesting information

2. I'd like to know/ask you if you would suggest that companies get rid of fringe benefits.
3. Would you mind telling me why a company provides a benefit such as membership of a health club?
4. Do you happen to know if/whether the company provided the benefits just because it was accepted practice?
5. Please tell me how we are going to take over control of fringe benefits.
6. Can/Will/Could you tell me if/whether each benefit achieves its purpose?
7. Do you happen to know how the organisation benefits from the fringe benefit?
8. Would you mind telling us how they administered the fringe benefits?
9. I'd like to ask (you) how our fringe benefits have grown without any control at all.
10. Can/Could/Will you tell us how much each feature costs?

4.2   Question types

1. direct/factual
2. encouraging
3. provocative
4. supportive
5. probing
6. controversial

5   *Word study*

5.1

1. disagree
2. insignificant
3. unincorporated
4. unimportant
5. improbably
6. inappropriate
7. inexpensive
8. illogically

5.2

1. optimism
2. minority
3. specific
4. illness/sickness
5. backward
6. negatively

UNIT 7

Appraisal and career management

Section A: Appraisal

Part 1: What is appraised?

1 Warm-up

1.1 Promotion and salary.
1.2 By providing feedback on performance and agreeing a plan for rectifying any perform-ance deficiencies.

2 Reading

In Chart 7.1:

a. Personality
b. Achievement of goals
c. Qualitative
d. Unstructured
e. Even-numbered
f. Scales

Chart 7.2

| | Measures | | | Method | |
	Personality	Behaviour	Achievement	Qualitative	Quantitative
BARS		✓			✓
BOS		✓			✓
MO			✓		✓

3 Comprehension/interpretation

3.1 They may leave important areas unappraised, and they are not suitable for comparison purposes.
3.2 One difficulty is that everyone defines them differently, and the personality traits that are used are not always mutually exclusive.
3.3 That factors beyond the employee's control may make it more difficult than anticipated, or even impossible, to achieve the objectives.
3.4 The job analysis.

4 Language focus

4.1 Expressions of frequency

2. As a result managers are occasionally promoted to positions in which they cannot perform adequately.
3. The usual/normal approach is the superior's rating of subordinates.
4. A group of superiors rating subordinates is also often/frequently used for appraisal.
5. A group of peers rating a colleague is rarely/seldom used in business organisations.
6. A fourth approach – subordinates' rating of bosses – is hardly ever/scarcely ever used.
7. Usually/normally/generally, appraisals concentrate on personal characteristics such as intelligence, decisiveness, creativity and ability to get along with others.
8. There are always pitfalls in carrying out appraisals.
9. Managers should never allow their personal biases to interfere with rating.
10. The employee should always be an equal and active partner with the manager throughout the appraisal process.

4.2 Both, either and neither

1. Performance appraisal is one of the most difficult tasks a manager has to carry out; neither the appraisal itself nor the communication of the results are easy.
2. Appraisal is the continuous process of feeding back information to subordinates about how well they are doing; it happens both informally and systematically.
3. In the case of informal appraisal the manager spontaneously mentions that a piece of work has been done either well or poorly.
4. Because of the close connection between the behaviour and the feedback on it, informal appraisal both encourages desirable performance and discourages undesirable performance before it becomes engrained.
5. A company's employees must see appraisal both as an important activity and as an integral part of the organisation's culture.
6. In most major organisations formal appraisals are carried out either once or twice a year.
7. To be effective, the appraisal method must be perceived by subordinates as based on both uniform and fair standards.
8. Managers should not allow either race, colour, sex or religion to influence their judgement.
9. Neither age, style of clothing nor political viewpoint should be allowed to interfere.
10. The halo effect is a common tendency to rate subordinates either high or low on all performance measures based on one of their characteristics.

5 Word study

1. P   2. Q   3. D   4. D   5. P   6. Q   7. D   8. Q   9. P   10. P   11. D
12. D   13. Q   14. D   15. Q   16. P   17. D   18. P

Part 2: Setting up the appraisal system

1 Warm-up

1.1 It is an opportunity for the appraiser and appraisee to go through the performance ratings or assessment, for the appraiser to explain the reasoning behind his judgements, and for each to give feedback to the other about their expectations and their concerns about the job.

1.2 Content that any criticisms made of his performance are justified, and that any courses of action agreed are the right courses of action to which he feels committed.

Listening tapescript

PB: Okay, good morning everybody. Shall we get started? In the last session we talked about what is appraised and we looked at some of the general problems associated with appraisal, such as qualitative versus quantitive assessment and behaviour versus goal achievement. Anyway, in today's session I'd like to consider how to set up a useful and workable appraisal system. Now, let's start by looking at the parties involved in this system. So, who is involved and interested in the appraisal process and its results?

P1: Well, there's the appraiser and the appraisee.

PB: Right. Anyone else?

P2: Yes, the organisation.

PB: Right, so those are our three interested parties. So, I'd like you now to divide up into your working groups of four, and spend just five minutes discussing the conditions that must be met from the point of view of, firstly, the appraisee, secondly the appraiser, and thirdly the organisation, if the appraisal system is to serve a useful purpose.

PB: So now if I could have some feedback from each of the groups. Simon, would you like to start?

P3: Yes, we said that one of the points was ease of administration.

PB: Easy for whom?

P3: Easy for the appraiser.

PB: Right, let's put that down.

P2: But, shouldn't it also be easy for the organisation to administer?

PB: Yes, go on.

P2: Well, it shouldn't cause any problems, I suppose, to any of the parties. From the point of view of the appraiser, there shouldn't be too much form-filling; there should be enough time allocated to do the job properly. From the point of view of the appraisee it shouldn't interfere with work routines; and from the point of view of the organisation it should provide information which is easy to access and interpret.

P3: But isn't that administrative efficiency rather than ease of administration?

P2: Yes, I suppose so.

PB: Okay, let's put up two separate points: ease of administration and administrative efficiency. Can we move on to another point?

P1: Yes, we spoke about fairness and relevance.

PB: To whom?

P1: To the appraisee. In the final analysis the appraisee should feel that any criticisms made of his performance were fair and justified.

PB: Right, so that's fairness and relevance. Anything else?

P3: Yes, we looked at the relationship between the needs of the present job and the needs of the organisation. We thought that the appraisal should address both issues so that there should be a fair balance between the two sets of requirements.

PB: Yes, can you say a bit more about that?

P3: Well, presumably there would be a difference between job achievement as narrowly defined and the goals of the organisation as broadly defined. And the appraisal should strike a fair balance between both sets of requirements.

PB: Good. So let's put up a fair balance between catering for job needs and organisational goals. Does that cover your point?

P3: Yes, that's fine.

PB: Good. Well, there's still a crucial requirement missing from the list.

P1: Objectivity.

PB: Exactly.

P1: The criteria that are assessed should be based on, or rather amenable to objective evaluation.

PB: Precisely. I'll put that down just as you said it 'amenable to objective evalutation'. Good. Now let's have a look at what we've got so far.

> Ease of administration
> Administrative efficiency
> Fairness and relevance
> A fair balance between catering for job needs and organisational goals
> Amenable to objective evaluation.

Any comments or additions?

P3: Is objectivity the same as job-related?

PB: Sorry, I'm not with you.

P3: Well, we said that the criteria should be genuinely related to the job.

PB: In what way related to the job?

P3: Related to the appraisee's success or failure in the job.

PB: I think that's a separate point from objectivity. What do the others think?

All: (murmurs of agreement)

PB: Is the appraisee always fully responsible for success or failure?

P3: No, because circumstances beyond his control may prevent him from doing the job.

PB: For instance?

P3: Well, if we tell one of our production workers to do something, and he can't because of the unavailability of materials or because the machines are not working properly.

PB: Good. Anyway, let's put down 'genuinely related to success or failure in the job'. Okay. Right, there's one more point which I think we should find. Any suggestions?

P2: Action plans or something about follow-up.

PB: Yes, go on.

P2: Well, as an example, if an appraiser and appraisee agree on a work plan for the following year or whatever, then the plans need to be monitored to check that they are carried out.

P1: But sometimes the plans aren't carried out, are they? I mean, sometimes they can't be carried out.

P2: Oh, they may need to be modified . . . if circumstances change.

PB: But, in any case, appraisal systems need to be supported by follow-up action: either through monitoring that what's been agreed actually takes place, or through modifying the action plans in line with changed priorities. Okay, I think that covers the main criteria for the criteria, if you see what I mean. Now next, what I'd like you to consider, is for whom each of these conditions is important – appraiser, appraisee or organisation. And, of course, the same point can be important to more than one party.

2 Listening

Chart 7.3

Conditions	Important to		
	Appraiser	Appraisee	Organisation
1. Ease of administration	✓	✓	
2. Administrative efficiency	✓		✓
3. Fairness and relevance		✓	
4. A fair balance between catering for job needs and organisational goals			✓
5. Amenable to objective evaluation	✓	✓	✓
6. Genuinely related to success or failure in the job		✓	
7. Supported by follow-up action		✓	✓

3 Comprehension/interpretation

3.1 Too much form-filling and not enough time.
3.2 Any criticisms made of his performance.
3.3 Unavailability of materials or machines not working properly.
3.4 Changed priorities.

4 Language focus

4.1 The language of meetings

1. b	2. j.	3. k	4. a	5. h	6. l	7. f	8. l	9. j	10. j	11. d
12. i	13. e	14. g	15. f	16. c						

4.2 Verbs of speaking

1. He told us that some managers rate each subordinate by different standards.
2. He talked/spoke to us about shifting standards.
3. He said that to be effective, the appraisal method must be seen to be fair.
4. Then we discussed the problem of personal bias.
5. He said to us how personal biases distort ratings.
   He spoke/talked to us about how personal biases distort ratings.
6. He said that an increasing number of organisations deal with the problem of bias by asking for explanations of ratings.
7. Then we talked/spoke about rating styles.
8. He talked about the different patterns of raters; some rate harshly, others rate easily.
9. He told us that the lack of uniform rating standards is unfair to employees.
10. We said to him that we thought it was also unfair to organisations.
11. We discussed how top management should integrate performance appraisal into the overall culture.
12. Finally we discussed how to make the employee an equal and active partner with the manager throughout the process.

5 Word study

Noun	Adjective	Adverb
use	useful	usefully
ease	easy	easily
efficiency	efficient	efficiently
separation	separate	separately
fairness	fair	fairly
relevance	relevant	relevantly
presumption	presumable	presumably
breadth	broad	broadly
success	successful	successfully
responsibility	responsible	responsibly

Section B: Career planning and management

Part 1: The stages in a person's career

1 Warm-up

1.1 Satisfaction, personal development, and an improved quality of working life.
1.2 Productivity levels, creativity and long-range effectiveness may be increased.

2   Reading

Growth stage
Exploration stage
Establishment stage
    Trial substage
    Stabilisation substage
    Mid-career crisis substage
Maintenance stage
Decline stage

3   Comprehension/interpretation

3.1   During the growth stage.
3.2   To develop a realistic understanding of his or her abilities and talents.
3.3   Early in the establishment stage.
3.4   Because many people are faced with the prospect of having to accept reduced levels of power and responsibility.

4   Language focus

4.1   Prepositions of time

1. after
2. to/till
3. In/During
4. before
5. on
6. after
7. during
8. at/during
9. at/during
10. at
11. in
12. in
13. at
14. until
15. by
16. for
17. in

4.2   Clauses of time

1. Before/When
2. before/until
3. When
4. as soon as
5. After
6. while
7. Before
8. When/While
9. Before/When
10. after
11. while/as
12. once/when

5 Word study

lives
stimuli
bonuses
curricula
indexes or indices
information (uncountable)
bases
criteria
analyses
appendixes or appendices
formulae or formulas
diplomas
beliefs
advice (uncountable)
mediums or media

Part 2: Identifying your occupational orientation

1 Warm-up

1.1 One's interests, aptitudes and skills.

Listening tapescript

PB: Okay, good afternoon, everybody. Shall we get started? In the last two sessions we looked at the area of appraisal, and some of the key areas associated with it, such as qualitative versus quantitive assessment, behaviour versus goal achievement, and how to set up an appraisal system. Our topic for this afternoon is career planning and the role of occupational orientation in it. The first step in planning a career – your own or somebody else's – is to learn as much as you can about their interests, aptitudes, and skills. People naturally seek out and excel in jobs that they are interested in and which they have the skills for. So the most sensible way to begin your career planning is by learning about yourselves. So, what I'd like you to do now is to divide into your groups and discuss your own personal orientation or orientations. Let me say that you'll probably come up with different features – perhaps even conflicting ones – but don't worry about that. So let's say fifteen minutes to discuss that, and then we'll have some feedback from the groups. Okay?

PB: Okay, let's see what you've all come up with. Sheila, would you like to start us off?
P1: Yes, well in my case there seemed or seem to be two orientations – firstly, I like working with data and I enjoy detail; that's the first point. Then I said that I don't have much patience dealing with people. I don't mind participating in training courses, but I'm not much good at training people myself.
PB: Okay, thank you Sheila. Anybody else who felt they liked working with data?
P2: Yes, I've always enjoyed working with data and working on problems – trying to solve them.
PB: Well, in fact you've mentioned two of our personality orientations. Firstly, there's what's called 'conventional' – which means people who like to work with data. They

typically have clerical or numerical abilities and enjoy carrying things out in detail or following through other people's instructions. Perhaps, Sheila, that explains what you said about instructing others. And secondly, George, what you mentioned about problem-solving falls within the category of 'investigative' – meaning people who like to observe, learn, investigate, analyse, evaluate or solve problems.

P2: Not sure about all the features, but some certainly apply.

PB: So what jobs do we have in these two categories? What about 'conventional'?

P1: Well, my field of accounts and bookkeeping.

P4: How about banking?

PB: Yes, those are some examples. There are more on the handout here. Let's look at 'investigative'.

P2: Yes, research and development, engineers – in fact all the scientific fields.

PB: Yes, exactly. Okay, so we've got two out of the six. Who's going to be next?

P3: I like to work with people.

P4: Yes, me too.

P3: But, I'm more interested in helping and developing them. Francis said he's more interested in persuading them. So I'm not sure if that's the same category. We thought it probably wasn't.

PB: No, in fact it is two categories. Helping and developing people is 'social' while influencing and persuading is 'enterprising'. The main difference is that socially-oriented people, like you Derek, enjoy using words, whereas enterprising people like you Francis enjoy leading or managing people in order to achieve the organisation's goals or for financial gain. Right?

P3: I see.

P4: That explains a lot!

PB: So, Derek, what kind of jobs do socially-oriented people go for?

P3: Secondhand car salesmen – they're good with words.

PB: In fact that is on my list. But, what others?

P3: Welfare officer or social worker.

PB: Yes, those are the types of jobs. That explains why you're in the welfare department. Now, what about the enterprising people, Francis?

P4: Well, sales personnel . . . and purchasing people.

PB: Yes, that's right. Okay, did anyone come up with anything else?

P5: Yes, I came up with art and design.

PB: Yes, that's the fifth category – artistic people – who like to use their imagination and creativity.

P5: So, that would include people in advertising, like me, and then people like musicians.

PB: Yes, exactly. All right, there's one more category to go.

P1: We haven't mentioned people with manual dexterity, have we? I mean people who like to work with their hands . . . either making objects or working on machines.

PB: Right, and that category is called 'realistic'. It's a bit broader than you said . . . people who have athletic or mechanical abilities, who prefer to work with objects, machines, tools, plants or animals, or to be outdoors. So people like engineers or farmers. Okay? Right, well those are our six categories. Now most people have more than one orientation and John Holland, who developed this model . . .

2 Listening

Chart 7.4

Personality orientations	Associated jobs
1. Conventional	Accounts, bookkeeping, banking
2. Investigative	Research and development, engineers
3. Social	Welfare officer, social worker
4. Enterprising	Sales, purchasing
5. Artistic	Advertising, musicians
6. Realistic	Engineers, farmers

3 Comprehension/interpretation

3.1 Clerical or numerical abilities.
3.2 Social and enterprising.
3.3 Leading and managing people.
3.4 Athletic or mechanical abilities.

4 Language focus

4.1 Likes and preferences

1. In today's session I'd like to look at career planning.
2. People naturally enjoy excelling in jobs that they are interested in and which they have the skills for.
3. First of all, you should divide into your groups and spend a little discussing your own personal orientation or orientations – in other words what you like doing.
4. Generally at that stage I like to get some feedback from the groups.
5. A: Okay, Sheila, would you like to start?
   B: Well, actually, I'd prefer not to.
6. A: Well, if you enjoy working with people, I think you would enjoy working in personnel.
7. In general I don't mind sitting in front of a computer; on the other hand I don't really like training people myself.
8. Well, we recognise two types of personality: 'conventional' people who like to work/working with data; they like other people to give them instructions.
9. On the other hand we have 'investigative' people, who prefer to observe others.
10. I don't mind other people helping me, but I prefer solving problems on my own.

4.2   Suggesting

2. How about kicking off with a brainstorming session?
3. Let's look at how to plan a career first.
4. I (would) suggest that you (should) learn as much as you can about their interests, aptitudes and skills.
5. I would advise you to begin your career planning by learning about yourselves.
6. So, first why don't you discuss your own personal orientation or orientations?
7. (I think) we ought to spend fifteen minutes on that.
8. He advised me not to train others.
9. How about trying banking?
10. Let's look at these in more detail.

5   *Word study*

1. to work on machines
2. to divide into groups
3. to learn about their interests
4. to look at the area of appraisal
5. to deal with people
6. to set up an appraisal system
7. to follow through instructions
8. to seek out jobs
9. to be interested in jobs
10. to come up with different features.

UNIT 8
The legal environment

Section A: Labour relations

Part 1: Trade union recognition

2 *Reading*

Chart 8.1

Why?	1.	To gain co-operation with employer
	2.	To gain benefits, e.g. employee representatives with whom to discuss, consult, and negotiate
When?	1.	Union has sufficient employee support
	2.	Sufficient support depends on:
		a. degree of union organisation and efficiency
		b. the size of the constituency
		c. the degree of opposition from non-union employees
For whom?	1.	That group of employees who have a sufficient commonality of interests, terms and conditions
	2.	This group is called a bargaining unit
For what?	1.	The terms and conditions of employment of the employees who are members of the bargaining unit
	2.	Possible range is anything in a contract of employment, but minimum is assistance by a union representative for members with grievances

3 *Comprehension/interpretation*

3.1   It limits management's decision-making power.
3.2   By considering union recognition claims more carefully and looking for ways of achieving collective consent by other means.
3.3   The competing claim for the recognition of another union.
3.4   Job; status and responsibility; frequency of payment.

4 Language focus

4.1 Review of modals

2. The step of recognition can/may be difficult.
3. There are cases where the employer won't agree to union recognition; in this situation the workers often won't co-operate with management.
4. In extreme cases this might/could lead to industrial action in support of recognition.
5. Recognition needn't be seen as bringing drawbacks to an organisation.
6. In fact employee representatives can/may often improve communication and working relationships.
7. Unions today must fight against the decline in union membership.
8. Employers needn't accept union recognition as the only way of securing the support of the workforce.
9. A union might/could be recognised with less than 40 per cent support.
10. A union can't be recognised without a degree of union organisation and efficiency.
11. A union mustn't seek recognition on matters outside a contract of employment.
12. Other agreements might/could take some matters out of the scope of union recognition.

4.2 Tense review

1. are recruiting
2. announced
3. have/has reacted
4. does not change
5. has/have recognised
6. (had) viewed . . . saw
7. were discussing
8. will be represented
9. were/are separated . . . would/will make
10. are still thinking

5 Word study

Verbs	Nouns
represent	representation
recognise	recognition
refuse	refusal
discuss	discussion
consult	consultation
initiate	initiative
achieve	achievement
maintain	maintenance
vary	variation
encourage	encouragement
consider	consideration
distinguish	distinction
employ	employment
antagonise	antagonism

Part 2: Conflict – sources, benefits and drawbacks

1 Warm-up

1.1 Wages, hours, and terms and conditions of employment.

1.2 By both parties through communication and negotiation.

Listening tapescript

Good morning, everybody. As I'm sure you know from your colleagues, every year I give a short talk about employee relations to those managers who have recently taken up positions with us as line managers. The purpose of the talk is to let you know the scope of your responsibilities as well as the scope of our – the personnel department's – support for your employee relations activities. I will come back to both of those points a bit later.

However, to put my talk into perspective I'd like to start by looking at conflict, and by presenting some observations on it. There are three questions I'd like to address. Firstly: what causes conflict? Secondly: what are the benefits of conflict? And thirdly: what are the drawbacks of conflict?

So, what causes conflict? It seems that we all have in us an aggressive impulse – a kind of innate drive. And although there are many pressures on us to restrain this drive, we all behave aggressively to some extent at some time or other. Some of the outlets for our aggression are vicarious – such as watching football, wrestling or boxing; but others are within our direct experience. And negotiations with our employing organisation are a splendid arena for the expression of combat.

The second cause of conflict is a divergence of interests between those classified as managers and those seen as non-managers. The first group is seeking principally, such things as efficiency, economy, productivity and the obedience of others to their authority. The members of the other group are also interested in these things, but are more interested in features like high pay, freedom of action, independence from supervision, and scope for the individual. And, as you can see, these, to some extent, conflict.

Thirdly, and more fundamentally, is the clash of values between the two groups. Values about how people should behave, about allegiances to political parties, about social class attitudes. And most frequently about managerial prerogative. Managers tend to believe that management is their right – and so can't be questioned, whereas non-managers tend to think that managers should be more open to questioning and criticism.

One of the most likely sources of conflict is the urge to compete for a share of the limited resources of the organisation – often seen as the money available for the payroll. Much of the drive behind differential pay claims is because one group needs to compete against other groups at a similar level to try and assert their position and status in the organisation.

The fifth possible source of conflict is tradition. There are some organisations and some industries which are conflict-prone. Fortunately neither the confectionery industry nor Codix has a bad record on industrial relations – and we would like to keep it that way.

Moving on. I've outlined five possible causes of conflict within an organisation – and the conclusion you might draw is that conflict is a bad thing – to be eliminated at all costs. However, that is not necessarily so. Conflict can bring some real benefits. And that's what I'd like to look at next – the advantages of conflict.

Well, firstly a conflict can clear the air by letting people get their bad feelings off their chest. By bringing a conflict into the open, the parties can start talking about their differences and start looking for solutions.

The second point is about rules – about new rules. Employment has a number of rules that govern it. Some of these rules are formal, such as the procedure for dismissal, while others are informal and unwritten, such as how we address each other. Conflict is one of the ways of changing the rules. Seen positively, it means that conflict is a creative process out of which change occurs. Now we all recognise that change is important, and that change can be good or bad. If conflict leads to a positive change, then it can and should be seen as a creative process leading to the introduction of new rules.

Just as conflict may be instrumental in changing the rules, it can also play a role in modifying the organisation's goals. Goals set by management may only be recognised as unpopular or really unattainable through conflict. Yet if this conflict is brought into the open it can lead to the positive step of modifying the goals in line with what is realistic. And through conflict this may be done earlier rather than later.

The final potential benefit of conflict is that it can lead the parties – the combatants – to understand their respective positions. Conflict brought out in the open leads to communication. And this communication about the issue enables the parties to see more clearly just what it is that they want, why they want it, and how justifiable it is. In challenging the position of the other party, they will come to a clearer understanding of where they stand, and why.

Of course, conflict clearly has its drawbacks. And the advantages that I've just mentioned need to be offset against the inevitable problems.

Firstly, there is the waste of time – and energy. There is a very real risk that the conflict can become destructive when over-personalised, and individuals become obsessed with the conflict rather than what it is about.

A second drawback is the emotional stress for the participants, and the need to be involved in lengthy negotiations is a source of stress which some people find very taxing, while others find it stimulating.

A third problem area is the organisational stress and inefficiency usually associated with conflict. Situations such as striking, working to rule, working without enthusiasm, withdrawing co-operation, or the simple delays caused by long negotiations.

Another drawback is the risk that when a conflict bubbles to the surface, it may not be resolved to the satisfaction of the parties and may become a thorn in the organisation's side, a recipe for future industrial unrest.

The final point is about communication and the vital role it plays in management practice. During conflicts, the quality and amount of communication is impaired, as the parties become more and more entrenched in their positions. The danger here is that this can lead to greater feelings of hostility as the communication worsens.

So that was by way of an introduction to our session. We've looked at conflict – its sources, benefits and drawbacks. In summary, what I think is important is . . .

2 Listening

Chart 8.2

```
                              CONFLICT

    1.  Causes
        a.  An aggressive impulse
        b.  A divergence of interests between managers and non-managers
        c.  A clash of values between managers and non-managers
        d.  The urge to compete
        e.  Tradition

    2.  Benefits
        a.  Can clear the air
        b.  Can lead to the introduction of new rules
        c.  Can modify the organisation's goals
        d.  Can lead the parties to understand their respective positions

    3.  Drawbacks
        a.  Waste of time and energy
        b.  Emotional stress for the participants
        c.  Organisational stress and inefficiency
        d.  Risk of future unrest
        e.  Worsening communication
```

3 Comprehension/interpretation

3.1 Watching football, wrestling or boxing.
3.2 For a share of the limited resources of the organisation.
3.3 The procedure for dismissal.
3.4 Striking, working to rule, working without enthusiasm, withdrawing co-operation, and simple delays.

4 Language focus

4.1 Comparing and contrasting ideas

2. Although some of the outlets for our aggression are external, others are within our direct experience.
3. The interests of managers differ from (those of) non-managers.
4. Non-managers are not as interested as managers in achieving efficiency, economy and productivity.
5. The values of managers are not at all the same as non-managers.
6. Despite the negative aspects of conflict, it is not a bad thing.
7. Conflict can lead to tension; however, it can also bring real benefits.
8. Some rules in an organisation are formal and written while others are informal and unwritten.
9. Despite the importance of change, change itself can be good or bad.
10. Organisations which actively try to resolve conflicts are generally healthy in comparison with those that ignore conflicts.

4.2 Toning down information

2. In a way, there are many pressures on us to restrain this drive.
3. We are just going to spend/We are going to spend just a little time on discussing the causes of conflict.
4. Our industry tends not to have bad industrial relations.
5. Maybe we should consider conflict as a positive force.
6. Conflict appears to have brought some real advantages.
7. To some extent conflict is one of the ways of changing the rules.
8. Conflict is inclined to waste time and energy.
9. Conflict taxes some people a little while others appear to become stimulated.
10. During conflicts communication tends to be impaired.
11. Perhaps this will lead to greater hostility between the parties.
12. So that was just an introduction to the session.

5 Word study

problem	conflict	govern	drive	status
drawback	aggression	rule	urge	position
disadvantage	clash	procedure	impulse	level

Section B: Employee health, safety and welfare

Part 1: The scope and importance of health, safety and welfare

1 Warm-up

1.1 Employers, employees, trade unions, government agencies and campaign groups.
1.2 Chance occurrences, unsafe conditions, and unsafe acts.

2 Reading

In Chart 8.3:

a. Health
b. Safety
c. Physical

Chart 8.4

To the employee:	1.	Lives and futures at risk
To trade unions:	1.	Rise in accidents
	2.	Hazards of new technologies
	3.	New diseases
	4.	Over six million workers in welfare and state sectors not covered by any legislation
To employer:	1.	Altruism
	2.	Days lost
	3.	Productivity and loyalty of employees
	4.	Fewer industrial relations problems

3 Comprehension/interpretation

3.1 Sanitation, canteens, hours of work, and rest pauses.

3.2 Counselling, improved communications, or anything involving the 'human relations' needs of people at work.

3.3 Because holidays are an entitlement within the contract of employment.

3.4 They are outweighed by production considerations.

4 Language focus

4.1 Subordinate clauses

2. Various authors have provided definitions which cover both physical working conditions and human relations.

3. Early authors wrote about workers' physical working conditions, including sanitation, canteens, hours of work, and rest pauses.

4. Early authors also developed the 'human relations school of thought', as/since/because they saw the achievement of job satisfaction as a way to bring about higher productivity.

5. There are two primary areas of benefit to the individual from the provision of welfare facilities, identified as physical benefits and emotional/psychological benefits.

6. If companies improved health and safety, then the workers' physical condition would improve too.

7. Although health and safety laws have been introduced, the number of accidents has continued to rise.

8. New diseases can be detected which are caused by working conditions.
   New diseases which are caused by working conditions can be detected.

9. Employers support health, safety and welfare provisions so that they improve/in order to improve workers' performance.

10. One director asked why the workers had taken industrial action when we looked after them so well.

4.2   Addition

1. *Wrong:* Health and safety are both aspects of employee welfare.
2. *Right*
3. *Wrong:* As well as providing physical benefits, welfare also provides emotional/ psychological benefits.
4. *Wrong:* They involve, too, the 'human relations' needs of people at work.
5. *Wrong:* The trade unions have also given it increasing emphasis./The trade unions have given it increasing emphasis also.

1. c   2. e   3. a   4. f   5. b   6. d

5   Word study

Noun	Adjective	Opposite adjective
health	healthy	sick/ill
safety	safe	dangerous
width	wide	narrow
height	high	low
reduction	reduced	increased
law	legal/lawful	illegal/unlawful
separation	separate	joint
satisfaction	satisfactory	unsatisfactory
generality	general	specific
decrease/decline	decreasing/ declining	growing

Part 2: When to report an accident

1   Warm-up

1.1   Management is responsible for making the workplace safe; the employees share in the responsibility if their behaviour is negligent.
1.2   Employees should be told and understand the nature of the hazards at the workplace; they need to be made aware of the safety rules and procedures; they need to be persuaded to comply with them.

Listening tapescript

SO: Now you've all seen this document before – it's our general policy on health and safety. As you know, every employer in this country is required by law to prepare a written statement like this. And all employees must be advised of what the company's health and safety policy is. My role as safety officer is to act as a kind of inhouse factory inspector, and part of my responsibility is to check that the policy is implemented. Now the purpose of this session is to look at one part of our health and safety provisions – reporting and recording accidents – and to tell you what accidents you must report. So what we are going to do today is consider in which specific cases you need to report and record accidents.

        First of all, when is an accident within the scope of the provisions? Well, what's the worst possible case?

P1: Death of an employee.

SO: Right. And below that on the scale?

P1: Sickness or injury of an employee.

SO: Good. So we're talking about death, sickness or injury. But to be within the scope, it must be connected to the workplace. It must result from an accident at work or from exposure in the work environment.

P2: Does that mean that we don't need to report or record any cases which don't happen at work?

SO: No, that's not quite what I said. I said it must result from an accident at work, not happen at work. So any injury or illness resulting from an accident away from work is not within the scope of the provisions. Okay?

P2: Yes.

SO: Now that's fairly broad, isn't it, if we recorded every case. So there are some limitations. Firstly, in the case of death, it must be automatically recorded. Secondly, any illness must be recorded.

P3: Is an illness a case that involves absence from work . . . and medical treatment?

SO: Yes.

P3: So where the company would receive a doctor's sick note.

SO: Yes. Now let's look at injuries. What injuries do you think need reporting?

P1: Well, first of all where medical treatment is required . . . so where we call in Dr Forbes.

P2: Does that include first aid?

SO: No, if Dr Forbes or the nurse says that only first aid has been given then it does not need to be recorded. So, that's the first condition . . . if medical treatment is required. What else?

P3: If the person loses consciousness.

SO: Right. Right, normally you'd call in the medical officer in that case anyway. But loss of consciousness must be reported. What else?

P2: What if the person can't carry on with their work?

SO: Not only with their work, but if the person is hurt and can't move any part of their body, then that needs reporting, too.

P3: What about if it is just a temporary thing? We'd normally call in the medical officer.

SO: If he thinks it's minor and only temporary, then you need not report it. And finally, if a person suffers an injury and has to be transferred to another job, that must be reported. Okay? So, we've looked at injuries which involve medical treatment, loss of consciousness, restriction of work or movement, and transfer. In any of these situations, the case must be reported. Is that clear to everybody?

All: Yes.

SO: If the injury does not involve any of these four, then it shouldn't be reported. So, now if you look at the total flowchart you can see quite clearly where you have to take action to report a case and where you needn't or shouldn't.

2 Listening

In Chart 8.5:

a. A death
b. An illness
c. Medical treatment
d. consciousness
e. to another job

3 Comprehension/interpretation

3.1 A written policy statement on health and safety.
3.2 He acts as a kind of inhouse factory inspector.
3.3 Those resulting from an accident away from work.
3.4 Those requiring a doctor's sick note.

4 Language focus

4.1 Like versus as

1. As you've all seen this safety report before, we needn't spend much time on it.
2. As safety officer, my job is to ensure that cases like accidents and injuries are reported.
3. The steps to be taken after an accident are as follows.
4. The first question is, 'Does it look like a serious accident?'
5. Such places as the washrooms and the canteen all constitute the workplace.
6. Accidents involving medical assistance like first aid needn't be recorded.
7. Some of you have been trained as first-aid officers.
8. As usual, there will always be exceptions to the rule.
9. If a person can't carry out their work as before, then the accident needs reporting.
10. As a precaution, whenever you are in doubt report the accident.

4.2 Questions types

1. Leading
2. Closed
3. Factual
4. Probing
5. Provocative
6. Controversial
7. Supportive
8. Closed
9. Redirected
10. Ambiguous

5 Word study

Noun	Adjective
death	dead
sickness	sick
injury	injured
health	healthy
safety	safe
accident	accidental
officer	official
responsibility	responsible
requirement	required
limitation	limited
provision	provided
connection	connected

GLOSSARY

A

absence (n) the state of being away from work

    absent (adj) not present; not at work; *it's your section head who will need to arrange cover if you are likely to be absent for a longer period*

    absenteeism (n) regular absence from work; *if motivation decreases, absenteeism is likely to increase*

accomplish (v) succeed in doing; *people are motivated to accomplish those tasks that they feel will definitely or are likely to lead to rewards*

accountable (adj) 1. responsible   2. having a duty to report; *he is accountable to the managing director*

    accountability (n) the state of being responsible

achieve (v) succeed in doing something

    achievement (n) 1. the successful completion of something   2. something successfully completed

action learning (n) learning by doing; *action learning involves giving middle-management trainees time to work full-time on projects, analysing and solving problems in departments other than their own*

ad (n) = advertisement; *we got a lot of response from the ad we put in the national press*

    classified ads (n) sections in a newspaper which advertise offers of jobs, sales, etc.

adjust (v) change slightly in order to fit into new job or condition; *new employees find they need to adjust to the company culture*

    adjustment (n) slight change; *nearly all employees receive annual adjustments to their pay*

adolescent (n) person aged between 13 and 16; not yet an adult

affirmative action (n) policy which provides opportunities for disadvantaged groups; *ABC company is an affirmative action employer*

aid (n) and (v) help

ambition (n) strong desire to succeed in life or in a job; that which is desired; *we try to give our employees an opportunity to fulfil their ambitions*

analyse (v) examine in detail

    analysis (n) detailed examination

    job analysis (n)

applicant (n) person who makes a request in writing for a job

    application (n) the act of making a request in writing for a job

    application form (Am.E.: application blank) (n) pre-printed form to make a request for a job; *application forms are used as a straightforward way of giving a standardised synopsis of the applicant's history*

apply (v) request something, e.g. a job, usually in writing

appoint (v) choose someone for something, e.g. a position or job

    appointee (n) person chosen for a position or job; *the appointee will need to work closely with all of you*

appraise (v) judge the value of somebody or something

    appraisal (n) calculation of the value of somebody or something; *qualitative appraisal often involves the writing of an unstructured narrative on the general performance of the appraisee*

    appraisee (n) person who is judged

    appraiser (n) person who judges; *from the point of view of the appraiser there shouldn't be too much form-filling*

apprentice (n) young person who is learning a skill

    apprenticeship (n) period of time spent learning a skill

aptitude (n) natural ability (to do a task)

arbitrate (v) act as a judge to settle a dispute

    arbitration (n) process of settling a dispute

assembly (n) the act of putting pieces together

    assembly line (n) layout of workers and machines where the work passes from one worker to the next, usually along a moving belt, until it is finished

    assembly workers (n) employees working on the assembly line

assess (v) judge the quality or quantity of somebody or something; *first we need to assess all the candidates in order to select the best ones*

    assessment (n) the act of judging the quality or quantity of somebody or something

    assessment centre (n) a method of selecting job candidates through group activities

attain (v) reach a goal; *if the reward is to be motivating, then there must be a reasonable chance that the worker can attain the desired standard*

    attainment (n) goal reached

bargain (v) discuss in order to reach agreement on something

    bargaining (n) act of discussing in order to reach agreement on something

    bargaining unit (n) group of employees who negotiate with their employers in order to reach an agreement

    collective bargaining (n) negotiations between unions and employers about working conditions, wages, etc.

basic (adj) normal; that on which everything else depends; *older workers will, of course, still be interested in basic pay*

behave (v) act

    behaviour (n) way of acting

    behavioural (adj) based on or related to the way of acting; *the personnel specialist might want to know something about the behavioural style of the supervisor and the members of the work group*

benefit (n) 1. advantage; profit; *many benefits are provided simply because it's the accepted practice*   2. money provided as a right under a state or private insurance scheme, e.g. disability benefit   3. (v) profit; gain advantage from

    fringe benefit (n) indirect payments provided by a company; *fringe benefits should be firmly incorporated within the payment policy and administered by the personnel department*

    sickness benefit (n) payments made while a person is on sick leave

blue-collar (adj) relating to manual work

    blue-collar jobs (n) *your local newspaper is usually the best source of blue-collar jobs, clerical employees, and lower-level administrative employees*

board of directors (n) group of people chosen by the shareholders to develop company policy

bonus (n) additional payment

C

candidate (n) person who puts him/herself forward for a job; *several managers normally interview one candidate because this increases the likelihood of making a good choice*

canteen (n) factory restaurant

career (n) job or profession for which one is trained and which one intends to do throughout one's life; *people have to decide how important work and career are to be in their total life*

    career development (n) the act of planning a person's future career within a company

chart (n) information shown in the form of a drawing or graphic

    organisation chart (n) a chart which shows how a job relates to other jobs and where it fits in the overall organisation

    process chart (n) a chart which shows in detail the flow of work from and into a job within an organisation

checklist (n) a complete list of items which is easy to use; *a checklist of critical questions has been prepared so that each candidate is asked for standard information*

clerk (n) person employed in an office to do routine tasks

    clerical (adj) relating to work done by a clerk; relating to work in an office

    clerical worker (n) person who works in an office

coach 1. (n) person who trains another person; *the coach works to improve the trainee's performance by discussion, exhortation, encouragement and understanding* 2. (v) train

    coaching (n) the act of training

collate (v) bring together and compare information in order to identify differences; *at the next stage these examples of behaviour are collated, and then returned to the raters without any indication of the scale point for which they were suggested*

communication (n) exchange of views and information either in speech or writing; *conflict brought out in the open leads to communication*

compare (v) look at several things to find similarities and differences

    comparison (n) 1. act of looking at several things to find similarities and differences 2. results of looking at several things to find similarities and differences; *appraisal is then based on a comparison between this and the performance actually achieved*

compensate (v) give something (e.g. money) to someone for loss or damage

    compensation (n) something (e.g. money) given to someone for loss or damage

compete (v) try to win; *one of the most likely sources of conflict is the urge to compete for a share of the limited resources of the organisation*

    competition (n) 1. act of competing 2. test of ability 3. other people or companies against whom one competes; *internal recruitment may not give a true picture of the real competition from outside*

competence (n) skill or efficiency; *if an organisation recruits from inside, employees see that competence is rewarded*

    competent (adj) efficient, able

condition (n) 1. general state 2. term of a contract

    conditions (n. pl.) situation; *it will probably be appropriate to start the interview with a neutral chat by asking non-controversial questions – perhaps about the weather or the traffic conditions*

    conditions of employment (n) terms of employment

conflict (n) disagreement; *conflict can clear the air by letting people get their bad feelings 'off their chest'*

consult (v) ask someone for information or advice

consultation (n) meeting to exchange information or to give advice; *changes in manpower utilisation often involve negotiation, or at least consultation with trade unions*

contract (n) agreement between two or more people which has the force of law

    contract of employment (n)

control (v) have directing influence over something

    control (n) influence or power; *there may be many ways of organising the pay packet that will facilitate control of operations and potentially reduce payment costs*

co-operate (v) work together harmoniously

core time (n) period of working day when all employees must be at work (*see also* **flexitime**); *however, you must all be here for core time from 10 till 3*

counsel (n) advice; (v) advise

    counselling (n) the act of giving advice to others; *emotional welfare stems chiefly from any provisions made to improve mental health, for example counselling, improved communications, or anything involving the 'human relations' needs of people at work*

create (v) make; *a new position has been created*

    creativity (n) ability to make new things; *that's the fifth category – artistic people who like to use their imagination and creativity*

criterion (n) (pl. -ria) rule by which one can judge something; *I'd just like everyone to be aware that we need to balance all these criteria*

current (adj) present

cv (= curriculum vitae) (n) written statement of education and previous employment; *if you want to apply, don't forget to send in a detailed cv*

deduction (n) money taken away from total pay for tax, national insurance, etc.; *if anybody has any questions about deductions, we can look at those after you've received your first payslip*

deficiency (n) something that is lacking or missing; *performance analysis basically involves verifying the fact that there is a significant performance deficiency*

define (v) describe exactly

degree (n) step in measurement; *sometimes on a five-point scale there will be four degrees*

demotivated (adj) not interested

department (n) part of an organisation; *the employment manager would like to talk to some of the company's supervisors and department heads*

develop (v) make something grow or increase

    development (n) act of developing or the result of developing; *training and development is a major feature of the personnel function*

discipline (n) training to produce self-control; (v) 1. train   2. punish; *face-to-face communicating includes interviewing, counselling and disciplining workers*

discontented (adj) unhappy

discrepancy (n) difference; *the first step is to identify the discrepancy between present performance and target performance*

disease (n) illness; *new diseases caused by working conditions are beginning to be detected*

dismiss (v) send away from/terminate employment; sack

    dismissal (n) act of dismissing; *these rules are formal – such as the procedure for dismissal*

division (n) main part of a large organisation; *the job description indicates where the job is to be carried out, e.g. in terms of location, plant, division, department, section*

DP (= data processing) (n) 1. the use of data by computers   2. computer department

drive (n) energy; motivation; *to succeed you need enthusiasm and drive*

duty (n) something that must be done; *in addition to identifying appraisal criteria, job analysis is used to formulate key tasks and duties*

earnings (n. pl.) wages or salary; *the absolute level of weekly or monthly earnings*

employ (v) take on or use a person as a paid worker; *during the year we employed an average of 65*

      employee (n) person taken on as a paid worker

      employer (n) person or organisation that takes on a paid worker

      employment (n) the state of being a paid worker

      employment agency (n) office that finds work for workers and workers for companies; *there are two types of employment agency: firstly, those operated by the government, and secondly, privately owned agencies*

engage (v) take on a person as a paid worker; employ; *let's imagine someone engaged in the manufacture of diamond-tipped drilling bits*

entitlement (n) a person's right; *income is linked to the notion of entitlement to a particular share of the company's profits or the nation's wealth*

      holiday entitlement (n) *in the United Kingdom holiday entitlement generally ranges from three to six weeks per year*

environment (n) surroundings; *to be classed as a work accident, the accident must take place in the work environment*

equal opportunity (n) no discrimination in terms of colour, sex, religion, etc. for employment

esteem (n) respect; *the work environment must also offer employees incentives for developing self-esteem*

evaluate (v) calculate the value of something; *the training and development manager plans, organises and evaluates training programmes*

      evaluation (n) calculation of value

expertise (n) particular knowledge or skill; *one of the advantages of using an employment agency is that it offers expertise in an area where the employer is not regularly in the market*

face-to-face discussion (n) discussion between people who are in each other's sight

feedback (n) information about the results of an activity, given to a person so that changes can be made; *the supply and demand forecasts need to be balanced and reconciled, and this process necessitates feedback into previous stages of the process*

file (n) collection of documents on a subject; *according to my files we haven't prepared a person specification for a team leader before*; (v) collect and store documents

fill (a position) (v) find someone to do a job

fire (v) send away from employment; sack; *our employment record is good in the community as we hardly ever fire anyone*

firm (n) company; organisation

flat hourly rate (n) fixed pay for one hour's work

flexitime (n) (*also* **flextime**) flexible system of working in which workers can choose what time to start and finish (*see also* **core time**); *with the flexitime system you can choose your start and finish time*

flowchart (n) graphic which shows information as a series of steps

fluctuate (v) rise and fall rapidly; *workers certainly don't want their pay to fluctuate wildly*

follow-up (n) action taken as a result of what was done before; *appraisal systems need to be supported by follow-up action*

forecast 1. (v) say what will happen in the future   2. (n) prediction

form (n) pre-printed sheet of paper on which to write information; *all job applications must be made on our application forms*

goal (n) aim; objective

go-slow (n) action of working slowly as a protest to management

grade 1. (n) step or level; score   2. (v) divide into steps or levels; *we've graded the applicants according to our preferences*

grievance (n) complaint made by worker to management; *the minimum level of union recognition is assistance by a union representative for members with grievances*

group selection method (n) method of selecting staff by evaluating their ability to work with others

guidelines (n. pl.) suggestions about how to do something; *union recognition involves the acceptance of a general framework of rules and guidelines within which management and employees operate*

hand in (v) deliver by hand

hand in one's notice (v) resign; *I've heard that three more are going to hand in their notice in May*

hazard (n) danger; *new technologies are continually being introduced that create new hazards not covered by existing laws*

head (v) be the head of; be in charge of; *the department is headed by me as personnel director*

health and safety (n) the measures taken by a company to protect its employees

hire (v) take on a paid worker; *make sure you hire people with the aptitude and potential to do the job*

HRD (= human resources development) (n) activities to develop the organisation's workforce

human resources (n) workforce of an organisation

       human resources management (n)

IT (n) information technology

incentive (n) something which encourages the workers to work harder; *incentive payments remain one of the ideas that fascinate managers as they search for the magic formula*

       incentive scheme (n)

income (n) wages and salary; *employees expect their incomes to be maintained and carry on rising*

induction (n) activity of introducing new employees into the company

   induction period (n)

industrial action (n) strike

industrial injury (n) injury which happened at work

industrial relations (n) relations between management and workers

industrial unrest (n) disagreement between management and workers resulting in go-slows and strikes

inefficiency (n) not able to produce good results quickly; *a third problem area is the organisational stress and inefficiency usually associated with conflict*

inflation (n) rise in prices linked to increases in production costs

initiate (v) start

inspector (n) person who checks the details or quality of something; *my role as safety officer is to act as a kind of inhouse factory inspector*

instalment (n) part; *the other eight days holiday may be taken in either one or two instalments, for example five days and three days or six days and two days*

insure (v) protect someone against loss, damage, injury or death by paying a sum of money

   insurance (n) protection against loss, damage, injury or death by paying a sum of money

integrate (v) join people or things together to form one single group

interview 1. (n) meeting to decide if a person is suitable for a job; *before closing the interview it is useful for the interviewer to summarise the key points and issues* 2. (v) conduct a meeting between an employer and prospective employee

   interviewee (n) person who is interviewed

   interviewer (n) person who leads the interview; *the interviewer should greet the candidate by name, and introduce himself*

inventory (n) list, especially of goods in a place

invest (v) spend money; *it's really for us to decide if we want to invest in a study*

job (n) piece of work

   job analysis (n) the process and results of collecting and analysing information about the tasks, responsibilities and the context of a job

   job analyst (n) person who conducts a job analysis

   job centre (n) office that finds work for workers and workers for companies

   job code (n) unique job reference consisting of numbers and/or letters; *the job code permits easy referencing of all jobs; each job in the organisation should be referenced with a code*

   job description (n) a written statement of what the job holder actually does, how he or she does it, and under what conditions the job is performed

   job grade (n) level or importance of a job; *the most senior job grades are shown at the top; and the most junior down here at the bottom*

   job mobility (n) ability to move from one place to another to take up or perform a job

   job rotation (n) movement between departments within an organisation; *job rotation aims to familiarise the trainees with the problems of each department*

   job satisfaction (n) feeling of contentment from doing a job well

   job specification (n) detailed description of what a job involves

   job summary (n) short description of what a job involves; *the job summary section should describe the general nature of the job, listing only its major functions or activities*

job-holder (n) person who holds a specific job

journal (n) newspaper or magazine

junior board (n) a junior version of the board of directors – the group chosen by the shareholders to develop company policy; *junior boards aim to give promising young middle managers experience in analysing overall company problems*

key (adj) important; essential

labour (n) work

    labour market (n) supply of workers available to work

    labour relations (n. pl.) relations between management and workers

    labour shortage (n) situation where there are not enough workers

    labour supply (n) workers available to work

law (n) rules made by government; *every employer in this country is required by law to prepare a contract of employment*

lay-off/layoff (n) action of stopping a worker's employment for a time, especially when there is little work to do

lead (v) manage; direct; *he is thus well qualified to lead this evening's session*

    leader (n) person who manages or directs

    leadership (n) quality or ability to lead

leave (v) go out

    leaver (n) person who leaves a company's employment; *on the top line we've got the leavers in the year*

legal (adj) made according to the law

legislation (n) law; *gradually other ways in which the employer could control wages costs are being eliminated or made more difficult by legislation*

liaison (n) contact in order to provide someone with information

location (n) place; position

loyal (adj) (worker) who supports his/her company; *loyal employees cause fewer industrial relations problems*

manage (v) control (an organisation or part of it)

management (n) group of people who control an organisation

    middle management (n) department managers

    senior management (n) top managers

manager (n) person who manages an organisation or part of it

    line manager (n) manager who is in charge of accomplishing the basic goals of the organisation

    plant manager (n) factory manager

    staff manager (n) manager who assists and advises line managers

manpower (n) total number of workers for a certain type of work or for an area

manpower demand (n) *manpower demand can be forecast using information from corporate plans or business plans*

manpower resources (n) manpower available

manpower supply (n) *the analysis of current manpower is essential as it provides a base from which to forecast the future internal manpower supply*

manpower utilisation (n) use of manpower; *changes in manpower utilisation often involve negotiation, or at least consultation with trade unions*

manual (adj) using the hands; *manual employees are usually represented by different unions from white-collar employees*

manual employment (n) *manual employment pensions are of growing importance in manual employment*

manual labourer/manual worker (n)

Maslow's hierarchy of needs (n) model of motivation which states that all an individual's physiological needs must be satisfied before higher-level needs, e.g. safety, belongingness, esteem and self-actualisation, can be fulfilled

measure 1. (n) action taken to achieve an objective   2. (v) find the size, length, amount, degree, etc. of something

medium (n) (pl. media) method of giving information; *the media include the local paper, a national daily or a technical journal*

mentor 1. (n) experienced person who advises and helps others   2. (v) advise and help others; *mentoring is similar to coaching in that it is based on a coaching/understudy relationship*

merit (n) quality of deserving reward

merit pay (n) merit pay is used as an incentive primarily for white-collar and professional employees

middle management (n) department managers

militant (adj) ready to support and fight for a cause; *the workers have rejected management's latest pay offer and have taken a militant attitude*

minority (n) small group (often suffering from discrimination); *this test has no cultural bias and is therefore not unfair to minorities*

mobility (n) ability to move

job mobility (n) ability to move from one place to another to take up or perform a job

motivate (v) give someone a reason or incentive for doing something

motivated (adj) encouraged

motivation (n) state of being motivated; *for motivation to take place, the worker must believe that effort on his or her part will lead to rewards*

motive (n) reason

N

negotiate (v) discuss with another or others to reach agreement; bargain

negotiation (n) (often plural) act of bargaining; *negotiations with our employing organisation are a splendid arena for the expression of combat*

notice (n) 1. information about something that will happen; *the workers gave the management 24 hours' notice about the strike*   2. information that a person will leave his employment (voluntarily or involuntarily); *I've heard that three more are going to give in their notice in May*

objective (n) target; aim

objectivity (n) state of not being influenced by personal opinions; opposite of subjectivity

occupation (n) job; *sometime during this period (hopefully towards the beginning – around 24 years of age) a suitable occupation is found*

    occupational (adj) related to a job; *during the period from age 15 to 24 a person seriously explores various occupational areas*

off-the-job (adj) separate from normal work; *off-the-job training takes place outside the actual workplace; in contrast, on-the-job training takes place in it*

on-the-job (adj) part of normal work; *important on-the-job techniques here include job rotation, coaching, junior boards and understudy assignments*

opening (n) job; vacancy; *if only two candidates appear for two openings, you may have little choice but to hire them*

organigram (n) diagram which shows the areas of responsibility in an organisation and the relationships between the personnel

organisation chart (n) diagram which shows the areas of responsibility in an organisation and the relationships between the personnel; *organisation charts show you how the job in question relates to other jobs*

orient (v) guide; direct

    orientation (n) 1. process of introducing new employees into an organisation   2. direction; *what I'd like you to do now is to divide into your groups and discuss your own personal orientation or orientations*

OTE (= on-target earnings) (n) often given in job advertisements as the target income, consisting of basic pay plus bonuses and other incentive payments

outcome (n) result; *the outcome of the interview is of great importance to the candidate*

outlay (n) cost; money that must be paid out; *the initial outlay to develop the orientation programme would be high*

output (n) quantity that a person or machine produces; *incentive plans usually result in greater output per man-hour*

overpay (n) pay someone too much

overtime (n) time after normal working time, normally paid at an extra rate; *however, at the end of any month you mustn't have more than 10 hours' overtime*

p.a. (= per annum) (n) per year; *the starting salary will be £24,000 p.a.*

part-time (adj) working for only part of the working day; *part-time employees now have to be nationally insured on exactly the same basis as full-time employees*

participate (v) take part in; *the workshop will be run again next month; so you'll have an opportunity to participate*

    participation (n) activity of taking part in

pay (n) money for working; wage; salary; *you will all receive your pay on the last Friday of the month*; (v) give what is due for services done; provide wages or salary

    pay claim (n) workers' request for pay increase; *much of the drive behind differential pay claims is because one group needs to compete against other groups at a similar level to try and assert their position and status in the organisation*

pay package (n) all the elements in pay, i.e. basic pay, overtime, bonuses, plus non-financial benefits

pay packet (n) wage, often in cash; *workers in the manufacturing sector can expect good pay packets when times are good*

pay restraint (n) agreement by workers not to ask for large pay rises

payroll (n) 1. all employees employed by a company   2. the wage bill of a company

peer (n) equal in position or age; *normally, everyone working in an organisation has peers with whom he shares information*

penalise (v) punish; *the assemblers are never praised for improving their output, nor are they penalised for poor quality work*

pension (n) amount of money paid regularly after a person stops work, either because of old age or illness; *another question might be: is £140 per week, plus a pension, better than £200 per week without?*

pep talk (n) talk to encourage a person to improve his performance

perform (v) do well or badly; *sometimes employees don't perform at the required standard because they don't know what the standard is*

> **performance** (n) action of doing something well or badly; *in the final analysis the appraisee should feel that any criticisms made of his performance were fair and justified*
>
> **performance analysis** (n) a method of establishing training needs through identifying the gap between current and target performance
>
> **performance appraisal** (n) procedure for evaluating a person's work
>
> **performance standard** (n) the required level of performance; *performance standards state how well the employee is expected to achieve each of the main duties and responsibilities in the job description*

perk (n) benefit given to a worker in addition to salary, e.g. company car, private health insurance

person specification (n) statement of the human characteristics and experience required to do a job

personality (n) nature or character of a person; *appraisal systems are sometimes designed to measure personality*

personnel (n) people employed by a company; *personnel management is directed mainly at the organisation's employees*

> **personnel policies** (n)
>
> **personnel record** (n) document, held by a company about each employee, giving personal and professional details

phase out (n) stop slowly or in controlled stages; *that's exactly why we phrased out perks at managerial level – they weren't appropriate*

picket 1. (n) striking worker who stands at the entrance to a company building to prevent other workers from entering   2. (v) to stand at the entrance to a company building intending to discourage other employees from entering

piecework (n) payment system based on the number of pieces produced

plant (n) factory

> **plant manager** (n) factory manager

pool (n) group of people; *the pool of women as a reservoir of inexpensive, temporary labour has decreased substantially*

position (n) job; *so this is a position between analyst programmer and junior project leader*

post (n) job; *this post must be filled as soon as possible*

potential 1. (n) person's innate capability for future development; *the organisation has an obligation to give every employee an opportunity to grow and to realise his or her full potential*   2. (adj) possible

praise 1. (n) commendation; *the supervisor's praise, which reinforces their good performance* 2. (v) speak well of someone

predict (v) describe the future

press (n) newspapers in general; *this post is currently vacant but we are advertising in the national press*

priority (n) first or most important objective; *in times of recession production considerations consistently tend to outweigh health and safety matters as a priority in management calculations*

probation (n) period of testing a new employee

    probationary (adj) relating to the period of testing a new employee; *the probationary period here is one month – I hope that you will all complete it successfully*

process chart (n) graphic which shows the flow of inputs to and outputs from a job

production (n) that which is produced by a company

    production figures (n) *business plans express the organisation's activity in such terms as production figures, sales figures, levels of service and so on*

    production worker (n)

productive (adj) producing well or much; *there is also a general feeling that employees whose health, safety and welfare are well looked after by the employer will be more productive*

    productivity (n) output level of worker or factory

profession (n) job for educated or trained person; *often (and particularly in the professions) the person locks on to a chosen occupation early*

profit (n) money earned by a company minus money spent

    profit sharing (n) system of giving the workers a share in the profits

progress 1. (n) movement forward; *finally, somewhere between the mid-thirties and mid-forties people often make a major reassessment of their progress relative to original ambitions and goals* 2. (v) move forward

project (n) plan

promote (v) give someone a better job; *up till now we've promoted the analyst/programmers to junior project leaders*

    promotion (n) act of giving someone a job with higher status

protégé (n) person chosen for a special task or job, and then helped and guided; *a protégé is chosen with especial attention to social background as well as professional skill*

punctual (adj) on time

    punctuality (n) ability or state of being on time

qualify (v) have the right education and background; *this course will help you to qualify as a member of the Institute of Personnel Management*

    qualifications 1. (n. pl.) required education, ability or experience 2. (n. sing.) result of finishing an education or training course successfully; *we are going to send Peter back to college, where he hopes to get a management qualification*

questionnaire (n) form consisting of a number of questions

rapport (n) close relationship; *at the first stage of an interview, the interviewer needs to make the candidate feel at his/her ease, develop rapport and set the scene*

rate (n) 1. amount   2. measure   3. (v) judge; measure

  rating (n) result of measuring something; *ratings can then be used to compare jobs for compensation purposes*

recognise (v) accept; *unions are recognised to some degree for at least part of the workforce*

  recognition (n) state of being accepted

recruit (v) take on a new person; *when a trade union has recruited a number of members in an organisation it will seek recognition from the employer in order to represent those members*

  recruitment (n) process of taking on new people; *so ads remain a good source of management recruitment*

redundant (adj) having lost one's job

  redundancy (n) state of having lost one's job

reference (n) written report on someone's personality and/or ability, often written by a previous employer

regulation (n) rule; *now under the present regulations a sick note is not required during the first seven days of absence*

reject 1. (n) something is not accepted   2. (v) turn down; refuse to accept

remuneration (n) pay

  remuneration package (n) all the elements in pay, i.e. basic pay, overtime, bonuses plus non-financial benefits

report (v) be under someone; *then there are four managers who report to me*

represent (v) 1. act for someone else   2. show; *these job codes represent important characteristics of the job, such as the wage class to which it belongs*

reputation (n) opinion held by others; *of course, whether high pay rates succeed in getting an organisation the reputation of being a good employer is difficult to say*

require (v) need

  requirement (n) what is needed; *the appraisal should strike a fair balance between both sets of requirements*

resign (v) give up one's job

  resignation (n) to give notice that you intend to leave a company; *to hand in your resignation*

retire (v) stop working because of old age or illness

  retirement (n) time when one stops working because of old age or illness; *as retirement approaches, there is often a deceleration period*

review 1. (n) survey; retrospective examination   2. (v) look at in general; *in the future we intend to review performance standards at least twice a year*

reward 1. (n) something given for good work; *the supervisor's praise may be enough of a reward to keep the assemblers' reject rates to a minimum*   2. (v) give something for good work; *your incentive plan should therefore reward employees in direct proportion to their increased productivity*

role playing (n) activity in which people play the part of others – often used as a training exercise; *towards the beginning of this period, role-playing is important, and children experiment with different ways of acting*

rule (n) something fixed by an organisation that a person must do; *employment has a number of rules that govern it*

S

sack 1. (n) dismissal   2. (v) dismiss; send away from employment

salary (n) pay, usually expressed as an annual sum and paid monthly; *for example, look at the wages and salaries you pay employees*

scale (n) system for measuring, divided into levels; *a form of scale is used, often comprising five categories of measurement from 'excellent', or 'always exceeds requirements' at one end to 'inadequate' or 'rarely meets requirements' at the other*

screen (v) examine in detail; *the time to screen out undesirables is before they have their foot in the door, not after*

> **screening** (n) process of examining in detail; *telephone screening can be used instead of an application form if speed is particularly important*

section (n) part of a department; *the personnel department is divided into five sections, each dealing with a specialist area*

select (v) choose

> **selection** (n) act of choosing
>
> **selection board** (n) group of people who choose a candidate for a job

self-esteem (n) opinion that one has about one's own value

semi-skilled (adj) of workers with some training

settle (v) agree on a solution to a problem

> **settlement** (n) 1. that which is agreed   2. a sum of money agreed as a wage increase; *a settlement of x per cent this year will set up an expectation of at least x per cent next year*

shift (n) part of the working day in a factory; *you need to decide some time before next Monday if you want to work the early shift or the late shift*

> **night shift** (n)

shop (n) place where products are sold or stored

> **closed shop** (n) scheme where only union members are allowed to work in an organisation or in certain jobs
>
> **open shop** (n) scheme where non-union members are allowed to work in an organisation or in certain jobs
>
> **shopfloor** (n) place where goods are produced in a factory; *my people all work on the shopfloor*
>
> **shop steward** (n) trade union leader elected by the union members

shortlist (n) list of successful people who go through to the next stage of a selection process; *here are the candidates whom we've shortlisted*

sick (adj) ill

> **sick leave** (n) absence from work through illness
>
> **sick note** (n) letter from doctor stating that a person is too ill to work; *if you are absent for longer, then you should arrange to see your doctor and ask for a sick note*
>
> **sick pay** (n) money paid during absence from work through illness; *younger workers are more interested in high direct earnings at the expense of indirect benefits, like pensions and sick pay*
>
> **sickness** (n) illness

simulation (n) training exercise in which imaginary situation is used to develop skills

skill (n) ability

> **communication skill** (n) ability to speak and/or write effectively to others
>
> **skilled employee** (n) worker who has had full training; *skilled employees are sometimes represented by a different union from the semi-skilled and unskilled*

specification (n) detailed description
  job specification (n)
  person specification (n)
  specify (v) describe in detail
spokesman (n) person who speaks for others; *I act as the main spokesman of the department and represent personnel issues in all our senior management discussions*
staff (n) people employed by a company
stage (n) period of time; step; *each person's career goes through stages*
status (n) position in a hierarchy
stoppage (n) act of stopping work because of a strike or breakdown of equipment
strategy (n) planned way to do something
stress (n) worry caused by difficulties; *a second drawback of conflict is the emotional stress for the participants*
strike (n) and (v) organised stopping of work
subordinate (n) and (adj) person below another in the company hierarchy
suggestion box (n) scheme for collecting workers' ideas to improve a company's operations
summarise (v) explain in short
superior (n) and (adj) person above another in the company hierarchy
supervisor (n) person who is in charge of others; *the supervisor will not be represented by the same union as the supervised*
  supervisory post (n) job which involves being in charge of others
supplier (n) person or company which sells to another person or company
support (v) and (n) help; assist; *each of these managers is supported by an individual or a small team*
survey (n) investigation; *recent surveys have shown that employers are reluctant to improve health and safety conditions*
System I (n) a model which states that managers mistrust subordinates
System IV (n) a model which states that managers have confidence in workers

talent (n) natural ability
target (n) aim; goal; objective
task (n) job or part of a job; *employees must also perceive they can actually do the tasks required*
team building (n) training activities to improve relationships between people who work together
temporary (adj) only for a short time or limited time
  temporary post (n) job for a limited time
terminate (v) end
  termination (n) ending of a job contract
terms (n. pl.) conditions, especially of a job contract
Theory X (n) model which states that people cannot be trusted to work
Theory Y (n) model which states that people do not have an aversion to work
time off (n) time away from work as a result of illness or other cause
trade union (n) group of workers organised together in order to bargain with management about terms and conditions of employment; *trade union recognition is widespread in Britain, although there has been a drop of over two million members since 1980*
train (v) teach or learn
  trainee (n) person who is learning; *the trainee works directly with the person he or she is to replace*

training (n) activities to teach somebody something; *a recent report on industrial training in the UK emphasised the great need for more and better training*

transfer (v) move to another place, e.g. a department

treatment (n) medical action to help someone who has been injured; *first of all, where medical treatment is required we call in the doctor*

turnover (n) 1. gross sales of a company   2. number of people who leave a company; *so the next point on the agenda is the turnover in the staff canteen*

understudy (n) person who is learning how to do a job from someone else so that the learner can take over the job in the future; *the understudy relieves the executive of certain responsibilities*

unemployment (n) state of being without a job

   unemployment benefit (n) money paid by the state to people without a job

upgrade (v) move up to a higher level; *we intend to upgrade some of the secretaries to assistants*

vacancy (n) job which needs to be filled

   vacant (adj) open (of a job); *one of the positions is vacant at present*

vacation (n) holiday

vocation (n) type of work that a person has an ability for

   vocational (adj) relating to work; *we have a strong tradition of providing vocational training for our people*

wage (n) weekly pay; *the wage rise last year was 7.5 per cent*

   wage freeze (n) decision by management not to increase wages

wastage (n) loss of workers through resignation or retirement; *manpower planners are concerned with trends of employees who leave the organisation, sometimes called wastage*

welfare (n) system of looking after employees; *health and safety are strictly aspects of employee welfare*

white-collar (adj) relating to office workers; *pensions and sickness payment arrangements beyond statutory minima are a sine qua non of white-collar employment*

withdraw (v) take away

   withdrawal (n) act of taking away; *the employee who feels underpaid is likely to demonstrate the conventional symptoms of withdrawal from the job*

work (n) doing jobs

   work sampling (n) system of measuring job performance directly

   work station (n) fixed place in a factory where a job is done, usually associated with a machine

   working conditions (n. pl.) general physical state of the place where people work, including things like noise level, hazardous conditions or heat

   working hours (n. pl.) the times of day or number of hours that a person works

   work to rule (n) agreement among union members to do only the minimum amount of work required by their contracts of employment

   workshop (n) 1. part of a factory where a specific job is done   2. a small factory